TO: Wendy

FROM: Mary

Matthew Emerzian teaches us that we are all important and can make a difference in the world. Read *Every Monday Matters* and learn how to be a giver rather than a taker!

—KEN BLANCHARD, coauthor of *The New One Minute Manager*®,
Servant Leadership in Action, and *Lead Like Jesus Revisited*

In sports, you have "All League," "All-American," even the catchall "All-Star" designation. Matt Emerzian is "All World" in the truest sense of the world. Armed with an innate curiosity, especially with regard to people, a deep inner compass magnetized for justice, peace and love, he humbly creates strategies anyone could follow in healing our planet.

—STEVE HAAS, Chief Catalyst Officer, World Vision United States

Matt Emerzian's latest is a must-read in our age of "me." An inspiring call to contribute our best for the benefit of all. It's the kind of book you pick up, start reading, and then put down, because you simply cannot wait to go out and do it.

—THOMAS GREANIAS, *New York Times* bestselling
author of the Raising Atlantis trilogy.

Matt's personal and compelling story was eye-opening to our management and employees, showing that we matter not only to one another, but to our customers, our communities, and our families. *Every Monday Matters* has been life-changing for me and many at our company.

—GREGG STRADER, EVP, Chief Banking Officer,
American National Bank and Trust Company

Matt taught me that my story of childhood homelessness wasn't about me anymore—it mattered, and I mattered because I had a voice to share my story when so many others haven't found theirs yet. And the guy wouldn't let me talk myself out of sharing it or leaving my law firm partnership to serve as CEO of Project Hope Alliance. Be careful—this book may have the same effect on you!

—**JENNIFER FRIEND**, CEO, Project Hope Alliance

With clarity of purpose and a loving heart, Matthew Emerzian promotes a mission of self-love, altruism, and the cultivation of meaningful connections… Matt gently guides us to gain a greater appreciation and understanding of our own unique gifts and our ability to transform our relationships, workplace, and world into a more kind, compassionate, and thoughtful experience.

—**ANDREW SHEPPARD**, Regional Director
of Operations, Sunrise Senior Living

I am so impressed by Matt's story and the life-changing programs Every Monday Matters (EMM) provides. The Jack in the Box Foundation has been proud to partner with EMM to help over a million young people discover why and how much they matter.

—**KAREN TRISSEL**, VP, Chief Insights & Analytics Officer, Jack in the Box

From the minute I met Matt and the Every Monday Matters (EMM) team at a conference three years ago, I've been inspired by their joy, their humor, the quality of their work, and their passion to support educators in living their lives with purpose. **Every EMM interaction, every article, every book, every product, exemplifies this passion and helps educators and others understand that they each matter and can make a difference—**Every. Single. Time.

—**HEIDI HAM**, Vice President, Programs and Strategy,
National AfterSchool Association

At Kiehl's, **we have a lofty goal—to positively influence every person we meet. And Matt Emerzian is the person who has taught us that this goal can indeed be achieved…** Want to motivate your coworkers to find true purpose in what they do each day? Look no further than Matt and Every Monday Matters. His passion and vision will unleash your potential, helping you and your team change the world around you for the better!

—**CAMMIE CANNELLA**, Vice President, Global
Education & Customer Experience, Kiehl's

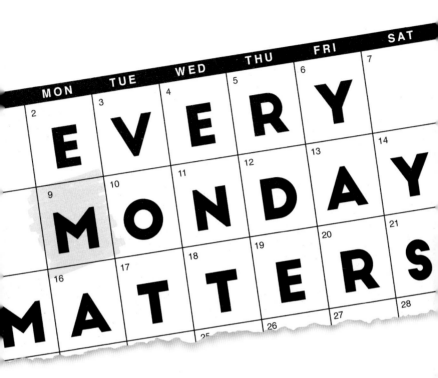

EVERY MONDAY MATTERS

HOW TO KICK YOUR WEEK OFF WITH PASSION, PURPOSE & POSITIVITY

MATTHEW EMERZIAN

simple **truths**

▶ Small books. **BIG IMPACT.**

IGNITEREADS

spark impact in just one hour

Photo Credits
Internal: page viii © Melpomenem/Getty Images; page viii-ix © Edu Lauton/Unsplash, Ji Pak/Unsplash, Kevar Whilby/Unsplash; page x-xi © Jon Tyson/Unsplash, Anthony Indraus/Unsplash, Swaraj Tiwari/Unsplash; page xiv © Chuttersnap/Unsplash; page xviii © Benjamin Sow/Unsplash; page 3 © Jamie Street/Unsplash; page 7 © Alejandro Alvarez/Unsplash; page 10 © Kanchana P/Shutterstock; page 13 © Soroush Karimi/Unsplash; page 17 © Bady Qb/Unsplash; page 20 © Edu Lauton/Unsplash; page 23 © Rawpixel/Getty Images; page 28 © Ann Kot/Shutterstock; page 30 © Marina Bakush/Getty Images; page 33 © Meredith Barcham/Getty Images; page 34 © Catrin Haze/Getty Images; page 40 © Ji Pak/Unsplash; page 43 © Nick Baker/Unsplash; page 47 © Simon Migaj/Unsplash; page 51 © Kevar Whilby/Unsplash; page 54 © Jenn Evelyn Ann/Unsplash; page 57 © Priscilla Du Preez/Unsplash; page 60 © William Daigneault/Unsplash; page 63 © Oliver Cole/Unsplash; page 68 © Tina Floersch/Unsplash; page 70 © Jon Tyson/Unsplash; page 77 © Sonia Bonet/Shutterstock; page 78 © Sergey201982/Getty Images; page 80 © Ryoji Iwata/Unsplash; page 87 © Jeremy Bishop/Unsplash; page 88 © Psphotograph/Getty Images; page 90 © Anthony Indraus/Unsplash; page 94 © Annette Shaff/Shutterstock; page 97 © Gianandrea Villa/Unsplash; page 100 © Boy Robert/Shutterstock; page 103 © Austin Chan/Unsplash; page 107 © Thiago Cerqueira/Unsplash; page 110 © Robertiez/Getty Images; page 113 © Nesa By Makers/Unsplash; page 117 © Freepik; page 120 © Swaraj Tiwari/Unsplash; page 124 © Rawpixel/Unsplash; page 128 © Trent Haaland/Unsplash

Published by Simple Truths, an imprint of Sourcebooks, Inc.
P.O. Box 4410, Naperville, Illinois 60567-4410
(630) 961-3900
Fax: (630) 961-2168
sourcebooks.com

Library of Congress Cataloging-in-Publication data is on file with the publisher.

Printed and bound in China.
OGP 10 9 8 7 6 5 4 3 2 1

For my wife, family, friends, and everyone in the Every Monday Matters universe who believes that a world where everyone knows how much and why they matter is possible. You inspire and matter to me more than I can possibly express.

CONTENTS

MONDAY GETS CONNECTED

MONDAY GETS AWARE

MONDAY GETS POSITIVE

MONDAY GETS EXPRESSIVE

MY STORY

I spent my entire life trying to be a success. More than anything, I wanted to know and show that I could be successful in that true Western culture sense of the word. I went to college. I went to grad school. I got a good job, and then I got a better job. I owned nice things, and then I got nicer things. I had the title. I had fun. Life was good. By all measures and outside perspectives, I was successful. Matt had made it. Just ask me, or anyone who knew me for that matter. But when I woke up on a Monday morning with a massive panic attack that turned into years of major anxiety disorder and deep depression, I quickly realized that my ladder of success was leaning against the wrong wall. I was sick and needed help.

Help can come in many forms. Trust me, I tried them all. I was game for anything I could do to feel better. But the truth is that I had a lot of work to do, and there was no easy fix. Kind of like how "success" wasn't the fix either. I had to completely shift the way I lived my life. I had to get uncomfortably honest with my self-serving and ego-driven ways. I had to own my shallow goals and reprioritize what mattered most to me. I had to establish new boundaries for myself and with other people in my life. I had to go to therapy every single week for several years and take antidepressants and Xanax—our world's newest vitamin. See, sometimes feeling better can't happen overnight, especially when what got us sick in the first place took years to develop.

But today, I am here to offer hope, and I am here to offer answers and suggestions, because my hope is that no one ever has to feel the way I did. For the past ten years, I have traveled the country sharing my story on stages in an attempt to help others. I have spoken to students, educators, employees, executives, criminals, veterans, victims of domestic violence, churchgoers, volunteers, and influencers—my message has never changed. I believe that we humans are all the same—we want to feel loved, that our life has purpose and meaning, that we are seen and heard, that we have gifts to offer the world, that we are worthy and enough, that our words and actions are meaningful, that we belong, and that we are good. In other words, we want to know that we **matter.**

INTRODUCTION

None of us chose to be born, but we all get to choose how to live. This is both good and bad news. Good, because it gives you a beautiful blank canvas to create whatever **master-piece** of a life you wish to create. Bad, because this places you right in the driver's seat of your own life. In other words, your choices, your words, your actions, and your thoughts actually matter in a very big way. This is where being human can be both mind-bogglingly awesome and a bit messy all at the same time. This is where my life went wrong.

In my desperate search to feel good, to feel accomplished, to feel like I mattered, I made all the wrong choices. Mattering can't be found in money, in social media followers, in material goods, in being popular, in fancy titles, or in corner offices. There is nothing wrong with having any of those things, but none of them are the reason why we matter, and this was the biggest eye-opener and life-changer for me.

I learned that all the answers I so desperately needed were only outside of myself. It was the day my therapist gave my recovery the motto "to live a life that wasn't about me" that my life truly began to change. It was my weekly dose of doing something for someone else—when all of the arrows shifted and started to point outward—that helped me truly start to find myself. I found myself in a weekly commitment of being in service to others. *What?* Mind blown.

Welcome to *Every Monday Matters*, both the nonprofit organization and this book. I believe that we can create a world where everyone knows how much and why they matter, and, in doing so, not only will our own lives change, but we will create a world like we have never seen before. "How?" you ask. It's simple…one Monday at a time.

This book is meant to be a guide, a Sherpa, that, when embraced by you, will not only change your life but the lives of people around you. Of course, life will always offer its challenges and seasons, but there is a deeper meaning to all of it that never waivers. It's when we are at our best as humans, living with a servant heart toward ourselves, others, and the world—that place where we matter most. Just as a weekly dose of mattering changed my life and the lives of millions of people in our Every Monday Matters world, I whole-heartedly believe it will do the same for you.

To make it super easy for you, this book is broken up into thirteen chapters. Each chapter has a theme—*Aware*, *Human*, *Kind*, *Resilient*, etc. Then, each chapter or theme includes four Mondays to help you engage in and experience the significance of each chapter or monthly theme. In other words, this book is best done one month or theme and one Monday at a time.

As you will discover, each Monday offers a mindful moment for you to read and process, then it provides several opportunities for you to engage. First, there are

HIGH, **MEDIUM**, and **LOW** engagement ideas. These are all about you taking action.

The back of the book also includes a journal-entry prompt and a conversation starter for each week. You will quickly see that this book is not meant to be completed alone. Of course, you are going to enjoy several personal and private moments throughout your time with the book, but get ready to involve your friends, family members, schoolmates, coworkers, and anyone else in your life who you would like to include. Remember, many of our answers to life's questions are found outside of ourselves, when we start to see ourselves as one connected humanity. The book offers plenty of cues to help you reach out and connect, so don't worry if that sounds a little scary or challenging—it won't be.

Get ready for the best year of your life. Get ready to feel good again and to have fun. And, mostly importantly, get ready to create a life that matters…one Monday, one action at a time. You matter.

> **Proceeds from the purchase of this book will be donated to Every Monday Matters to support its national YOU MATTER™ K-12 Education Program, helping millions of youth embrace how much and why they matter. To learn more, visit everymondaymatters.org.**

MONDAY GETS INTROSPECTIVE

Billions of dollars are spent each year by people searching for answers to all of life's big questions. We buy books like this one, go to seminars and retreats, employ life coaches, watch videos—all in an effort to find "it." The fact that so many of us are spending our time, money, and energy on quests for personal growth, transformation, and Zen-ness must mean there are a lot of us out there feeling as though something is missing. On one hand, this is a little bit sad, but it is also inspiring and hope-provoking. We believe deeply that there is something better and more to life. Even when we don't feel like it, we do our best to show up every day in our pursuit of fixing the holes in our hearts and finding true meaning and purpose in our lives. Well, we can and we will. It just takes a little patience, perspective, and persistence. Individually—and together—we can find the love and peace we all so deeply yearn for, so get ready for an awesome month. Being introspective matters.

THIS WEEK...
SEARCH YOUR SOUL

We are taskmasters, multitaskers, to-do-list killers, and get'er-doners. We thrive at checking things off...or at least we think we do. I think we have lost something in all of our doing. We have become "human doings," leaving our "being" at the door of life, and this ignores so much of what makes us human. So this week, your to-do list only has one item on it: **SEARCH YOUR SOUL**. Checking in with ourselves doesn't always come easy. It's our soft underbelly. So start by asking a few questions: What makes you happy and healthy? What challenges are you facing right now? How are your relationships going? What do you care about, and how much time do you spend on the things that matter most to you? What is one thing you want to change or improve about yourself or your life? What drives you crazy?

Don't be timid; this is good stuff. It's really worth sorting it out and spending time on. Our souls are complex and fragile. They need and deserve our attention, and there is no better time than the present to search them. Enjoy the process. Searching your soul matters.

TAKE ACTION

HIGH: Create a "soul pizza." Draw a circle divided into eight slices. Label each slice with aspirations, like "Health," "Fun," "Work," etc. Color to your status. For example, color half the slice if you are about 50 percent of where you want to be for "Health." Use as a guide to grow!

MEDIUM: Plan some regular soul time. Maybe it is five minutes before falling asleep, taking a long walk every Saturday morning, or journaling at lunch. The key is to create some space to really check in with yourself. You'll be surprised at how much you begin to enjoy it!

LOW: What's something you really miss in your life that you know is soulful and soul-filling? Now go do it. No excuses.

> **WHAT IS A SOUL? IT'S LIKE ELECTRICITY— WE DON'T REALLY KNOW WHAT IT IS, BUT IT'S A FORCE THAT CAN LIGHT UP A ROOM.**
>
> —Ray Charles

HAVE A DREAM

TAKE ACTION

HIGH: Create a "share your dreams" wall in a common area in your home or at work, and invite people to write or draw one or more of their dreams for the year on it. Sharing our dreams connects us and increases the likelihood of them becoming a reality.

MEDIUM: Start a dream journal. Write down your dreams for the year, and journal about your journey of accomplishing them. When a new dream comes to you, add it to your journal and keep plugging away throughout the year. Note: this is *not* a sleep journal.

LOW: Pick three words...or four or five. Think of words that embody your hopes and dreams. Instead of simply writing down the first three words that automatically pop into your mind, think a bit harder, then write them down. Hold those words close to your heart as you dream away.

> I ONLY HOPE THAT WE NEVER LOSE SIGHT OF ONE THING—THAT IT WAS ALL STARTED BY A MOUSE.
>
> —Walt Disney

We have all heard or heard of Martin Luther King Jr.'s "I Have a Dream" speech. Search any "Best Speeches of All Time" lists, and I guarantee it is on there. Beyond the boldness and the beauty of his dream and his 1963 speech, what is arguably even more astounding is the fact that he single-handedly created a dream that day for millions of people that—over fifty years later—we are still pursuing. That is the power of dreams. So what do you dream about…for yourself, your friends and family, your community, and the world? It's time to **HAVE A DREAM**. Maybe it is something bigger than you have ever taken on before. Or maybe it is less about building up to something big and more about making small shifts or changes in your life that make all the difference. Either way, making your dreams a reality will require your focus, energy, and effort, but never forget that it all starts with a dream. So use this week to get in touch with your heart, your desires, and your hopes, then create your vision. It's all possible. Having a dream matters.

THIS WEEK...
BE IN AWE

Think for a minute. Think about something that literally took your breath away. Maybe it was winning your first trophy, dancing at your wedding, or watching your child take their first steps. When moments like these happen, life couldn't get any better. We feel joy. We smile on the inside and out, and we experience a sense of warmth and wonder. But does it always have to be a first in order for us to feel this utter joy and completeness? I don't believe so. So this week, we are all going to **BE IN AWE**. Sure, there are some big and awesome moments in life, but what about all the ones in between? We are surrounded by awe-inspiring moments each and every day—a hug from a friend at the perfect moment, the blooms of spring wildflowers, a heartfelt compliment. See, we are surrounded by awesomeness; we just need to do a better job of seeing and feeling the awe part. For every single time our hearts beat and our lungs fill with air, we are given that miracle to feel awe all over again. So be sure to take it all in. Being awestruck matters.

TAKE ACTION

HIGH: Host an awesome art party! Provide a variety of materials that your invitees can use to create visuals of what brings awe to their lives. It may be sunsets, kittens, inspirational quotes, stories, or something more abstract like a feeling or certain colors and shapes. Showcase the awesome when done!

MEDIUM: Perfect your skill of seeing and feeling awe. Start in the morning when you first wake up, and continue throughout your day. As the awesomeness unfolds, take a moment to connect and even consider writing each awesome moment down. All awesome events, big and small, are welcome.

LOW: Be the one who points out the awe every day. "Did you see…?" "I am awestruck whenever…" "You are awesome when you…" Go. Be *that* person. Just know that your awesome gestures may be contagious.

> ## MIRACLES COME IN MOMENTS. BE READY AND WILLING.
>
> —Wayne Dyer

LIVE AUTHENTICALLY

TAKE ACTION

HIGH:. The next time you are not feeling your best, share it on social media. *Yikes.* I know. But you might just discover that you're not the only person not feeling so great that day, and you will have inspired authenticity in others—a real human highlight reel for a change.

MEDIUM: Think about a time when someone asked you how you were feeling and you weren't 100 percent honest in your response. Or when you said anything was good for lunch and ended up with food you didn't care for. Well, no longer! It's time to be honest in all situations.

LOW: Choose to be 110 percent yourself today. Even if you only take a few baby steps by being true to yourself, you'll be surprised at how good it feels to finally honor who you are on the inside with your words and actions on the outside.

> LIVE AUTHENTICALLY. WHY WOULD YOU CONTINUE TO COMPROMISE SOMETHING THAT'S BEAUTIFUL TO CREATE SOMETHING THAT IS FAKE?
>
> —Steve Maraboli

Everyone likes the real deal. We don't want #fake. We don't want dishonesty. We want the truth. However, no matter how much we believe we need it, the truth is we're not so great at it. We lie to ourselves, we hide our flaws, and we put on that fake smile even when we're not feeling it. Living this way is not good for us individually, and it's an absolute deal-breaker for relationships. If we can't be true to ourselves, how can we grow, thrive, or be true with others? We can't, so let's **LIVE AUTHENTICALLY**. Our world is in dire need of what's real rather than the abstract, subjective, and outright false. We need to take ownership of our actions and everything that makes us *us*. No more highlight reels on social media. Let's step out—with all our imperfections—and lovingly share empathy and acceptance with ourselves and everyone else. Doesn't that sound better already? Yes, it's a two-way street. So let's not judge, and if someone does, then encourage them to join you in being their true self. Be your true you, because *you* matter. Being authentic matters.

MONDAY GETS AMBITIOUS

If we want things to change, we have to change. It's that simple. Change doesn't just happen on its own. It is on each of us to make it happen. We can no longer afford apathy, finger pointing, the victim mentality, or the blame game. We just need to start owning our power, because each and every one of us matters. Our words, our actions, and our thoughts all matter and have lasting ripple effects. Knowing this is powerful, but owning it is life- and world-changing. So get ready to get in the game. Nothing happens when we just sit on the sidelines. Same goes for living a full life or creating a better world. We all have what it takes. There is nothing to be afraid of and nothing new to learn. We all know plenty already. We just need to step up and make it happen. If we want more love in our lives and the world, then let's start being more loving. The same goes for kindness, respect, hope, friendship, goodness, generosity, and joy. It is up to us to create them. So get ready. Buckle your seatbelt. It starts with you. Being ambitious matters.

THIS WEEK...
PLAN YOUR PLAN

Have you ever sat down and truly made a plan for your own life? Have you set your goals for the next five years, one year, month, or even next week? We have all heard the saying "People don't plan to fail; they fail to plan," but how many of us have actually taken it to heart? Do we just float through our routines and life instead? Being ambitious is a great place to start, but without a plan, we will never achieve our goals or mission. So this week, it's time to **PLAN YOUR PLAN**. Plans come in all shapes and sizes, but they always start with a goal. Maybe it is greater financial stability or going back to school. Maybe it is a goal to improve your health or develop stronger friendships. Through goals, we can then work backward and develop a step-by-step plan to achieve them. We might even discover some potential pitfalls as we get a better understanding of what our goal is going to take to achieve. And let's remember that we already subject ourselves to enough performance pressure, so let's make this a healthy and successful experience. Planning your plan matters.

> **IT TAKES AS MUCH
> ENERGY TO WISH AS
> IT DOES TO PLAN.**
>
> —Anonymous

TAKE ACTION

HIGH: Let's think big. Pick one area of your life for which you want to set a new and ambitious goal, then write down your one-year, three-year, five-year, and even ten-year achievement goals. Now outline the steps and create the plan you'll need to achieve each major milestone along your journey.

MEDIUM: Set a goal and create a plan for something you've always wanted to do and can realistically achieve within one year. Consider it a practice run for something even more ambitious.

LOW: Think of a time when you set a goal for yourself, created a plan, and then made it happen. What a rush! Hold onto that feeling as you get ready to set a new goal, make a plan, and put positive personal change into motion.

FAIL AT SOMETHING

TAKE ACTION

HIGH: Start a newbie group with your family, friends, or coworkers. Have everyone share three things they have always wanted to try with the group. Support one another in being a newbie! You may find you are not the only person wanting to run a marathon or learn how to crochet.

MEDIUM: Do something this week that you know you will not be good at. Paint, try a climbing wall, or learn sign language and try to use it after just one lesson. Pick something you know you can't do, and accept that you won't be perfect right out of the gates.

LOW: Next time you're at lunch with a few friends or eating dinner with the family, swap failure stories. These stories can be about your personal experiences or the failures of famous people throughout history. See if you can find the lesson or silver lining in the midst of these failures.

> **I CAN ACCEPT FAILURE; EVERYONE FAILS AT SOMETHING. BUT I CAN'T ACCEPT NOT TRYING.**
>
> —Michael Jordan

Being new at something is an interesting thing. As children, we were amazing at it, because we experienced something new every single day. On the other hand, as adults we have a little bit of the "been there, done that" mentality. After all, we've been alive longer, so we've already tried and discovered everything, right? I say, "Wrong." The world offers way more than any of us could experience in one lifetime. So this week, let's **FAIL AT SOMETHING**. We now live in the day of #EpicFail. In other words, failing is bad. But is it really? I'm not convinced it is. Scientists spend their entire lives proving themselves wrong in order to get one step closer to the truth. Failing means that we went after something, that we tried something new without really knowing how things were going to turn out. And that was OK, because we knew we would still learn something. Isn't that freeing? We all need to embrace the fact that we can't fail unless we try, and we can't succeed without failing. Maybe the biggest failure is to never try. So get ready to try and fail, then do it again. Failing at something matters.

THIS WEEK...

GET ENERGIZED

There are varying degrees to our ambitions. Some of them might be the "Oh, that would be nice if..." type, and others are more of the "I am all-in and going to go after this" type. I think there is an argument for both, but this week is all about the latter. When we decide in our head and in our heart that we want something, we better know one thing for sure—it's going to take energy and, most likely, a lot of it. Pursuing our dreams requires a delicate balance of expending and refueling. So this week, we are going to **GET ENERGIZED**. What fires you up? What gets your body, mind, and soul ready to bring it? Coffee doesn't count. Are you exercising, eating right, reading good books, getting enough rest, and spending quality time with people who lift you up? Well, now is the time, because in pursuit of our goals, we will face setbacks, fears, and even naysayers. But we can't let these deflate or defeat us. Rather, we will refuel and welcome a new day, filled with focus, inspiration, and energy. So get pumped up and ready for your marathon. Getting energized matters.

WHERE I GET MY ENERGY IS: "HOW CAN I MAKE IT BETTER?"

— Sara Blakely

TAKE ACTION

HIGH: Create a "get energized" morning routine for yourself. What are one to three things you can do each morning to start your day off pumped up? Pick them, then do them…every single morning. And don't be afraid to change or step them up every so often.

MEDIUM: Spend time with people who naturally energize you, and find simple ways to do things together to foster that energy. Imagine you're a posse of Energizer Battery bunnies beating on that drum. Look at you go…and go…and go.

LOW: Create a list of activities that increase or decrease your energy on dual sides of a piece of paper. Once completed, commit to spending more time doing the activities that add energy while reducing your time wasting energy. Feel better already?

BE YOUR OWN BIGGEST FAN

TAKE ACTION

HIGH: Create a "Walk of Fame" with your coworkers, friends, or family members. Have each person decorate the paper (or star!) with their name and all the things that make them special and amazing. Once done, line up the papers and walk together— cheering and applauding each in support!

MEDIUM: Notice if there are people in your life who don't believe in themselves or have low confidence. Then, sign up to be their fan without telling them. Show how much they have to offer the world through actions, and reinforce how much you appreciate them for who they are.

LOW: Start an "I matter" journal, and fill it with positive statements that you believe people would say about you or you believe yourself. No one will read it but you, so don't be modest. Keep adding to your list and embrace how awesome you are!

> # YOU HAVE TO BELIEVE IN YOURSELF WHEN NO ONE ELSE DOES— THAT MAKES YOU A WINNER RIGHT THERE.
>
> —Venus Williams

Remember when you were too small to ride on certain roller coasters? You waited for hours in line to finally stand next to the outreached paw or finger of a wooden Roadrunner or Batman, only to learn you weren't tall enough to go on the ride. Unfortunately, we have all had several experiences throughout our lives where we were told or felt like we weren't enough. It's almost like the word *enough* comes with an empty blank in front of it that we fill in again and again over the years. And with every new enough combo added to our lists, our self-worth is slowly whittled away. Well, enough of that. It's time for you to **BE YOUR OWN BIGGEST FAN**. You are an incredible person. You are one in over seven billion—that's pretty impressive. So know in your heart how much you matter. Know that you have all it takes—and more—to accomplish whatever it is you want to accomplish. Of course, it is going to take a little bit of courage, love, and support, but it all starts with your belief in yourself. Go conquer the world. Being your own biggest fan matters.

MONDAY GETS JOYFUL

There is something pretty awesome that the words *cheerful*, *happy*, *jolly*, *merry*, *blissful*, *upbeat*, and *radiant* have in common. They are all synonyms for the word *joyful*. Even more joyful than that, there is also an endless supply of joy, and it can be shared and experienced in so many forms. Now we're talking. But sometimes finding joy can feel a bit distant and beyond our reach. Maybe we have become jaded and cynical. Or maybe we forgot what a good belly laugh feels like or the sense of pride we experienced when we got our driver's licenses. Well, get ready for a big dose of joy this month, because we are surrounded by it everywhere, and we are about to create even more of it. We can feel it in the words of a handwritten note. We can feel it in a hug from a dear friend. We can see it in the trees as the fall leaves change colors. Don't even bring up puppies and kittens… That's not fair. It's time to witness the contagious power of joy. Being joyful matters.

PLAY MORE

How is it that growing up has become synonymous with growing serious...more responsibilities, judgment and awareness of other people's judgments, skepticism, and know-it-all-ness? But does this really need to be the case? After all, who ever said that being happy, laughing, or expressing your inner-nerd or childlike ways has an expiration date? I certainly didn't. So this week, let's all agree to **PLAY MORE**. The word *play* is defined as "to engage in activity for enjoyment and recreation rather than a serious or practical purpose." Wait, for "enjoyment and recreation"? Doesn't that sound fun and refreshing? There is a question that we all used to ask as children, and it's time to bring it back this week: "Can you play today?" I don't care how young or old you are, because this question needs to become a larger part of our lives again. Playing is good for the soul. It's good for our relationships. It's good to step out of our "stuff" for a little while to just let go. Life is meant to be enjoyed...at least most of the time. So let's get a little playful this week. Playing matters.

YOU CAN DISCOVER MORE ABOUT A PERSON IN AN HOUR OF PLAY THAN IN A YEAR OF CONVERSATION.

—Anonymous

TAKE ACTION

HIGH: Start a hobby that looks downright fun. You now have the green light to start. But be warned: you might not be very good at it in the beginning, so don't get frustrated or let that suck the joy out of it for you. Remember, you are playing.

MEDIUM: Set a weekly or monthly playdate with a friend or group of friends. Let every member of the group pick the activity for any given playdate. This will ensure new adventures ahead for everyone, which is a big part of playing.

LOW: We have all heard the saying "Sing, dance, and laugh like no one is watching." Well, who cares if someone is watching? We shouldn't. So go sing, dance, and laugh away.

LAUGH TILL IT HURTS

TAKE ACTION

HIGH: Plan a laughter night with friends, family, or coworkers. Ask everyone to bring something that makes them laugh and will surely get the group laughing. Maybe it is a game, their favorite joke, or their favorite YouTube video. Have fun laughing till it hurts.

MEDIUM: Find a funny picture, daily cartoon, or anything else that will make someone laugh. Not just smile but really laugh. Plant them in all of their frequently visited places, including their car, office, bedroom, etc. Then prepare to enjoy with them as you hear them discover their little surprises.

LOW: Put some time aside every day to do whatever it is that makes you laugh freely. It can be as little as five minutes if that's all the time you have. But don't settle for anything less than that. Find some time each day to laugh, then laugh some more!

> IF YOU LAUGH, YOU THINK, AND YOU CRY, THAT'S A FULL DAY. THAT'S A HECK OF A DAY. YOU DO THAT SEVEN DAYS A WEEK, YOU'RE GOING TO HAVE SOMETHING SPECIAL.
>
> —Jim Valvano

If I told you there is something you can do as many times a day as you want and it reduces stress, lowers your blood pressure, works out your stomach muscles, improves your heart health, boosts T cells, releases endorphins, burns calories, and improves your general sense of well-being, would I get your attention? What if I also told you that it positively impacts the people around you and doesn't involve starving or exercise? Now would I have your attention? Good, because this week we are going to **LAUGH TILL IT HURTS**. We are obsessed with staying happier and younger longer. We've tried the Lucky Strike diet, the grapefruit diet, the cabbage soup diet. We went fat free, we Jazzercised, and we even SlimFasted and Weight Watched. Well, there is a new program I am claiming right now: the laughing diet. Dare I say it just might be the real fountain of youth? No furrowed brows allowed on this program, though. Nothing but fun and amazing benefits. All we need to do is hand it over, crack ourselves—and others—up, and enjoy feeling good. Have a blast. Laughing till it hurts matters.

ADD COLOR

Adults make over 35,000 choices every day. Assuming seven hours of sleep, that's 2,058 choices per waking hour or 34 per minute. Of all those choices, do we ever take a moment to intentionally decide on how we want to show up in the world at any given moment or on any given day? Because our presence alone instantly changes the dynamic. Why? Because we are there. The question then is a matter of what we are choosing to bring to any of these situations. Well, in the spirit of this month being about joy, I hope it is something uplifting, inspiring, and positive. So this week, get ready to **ADD COLOR**. There is a reason we don't have black-and-white screens any more...because life is colorful and a colorful world is more engaging. Color adds dimension and personality, and it even affects our moods. So what color do people get from you? In other words, what impact do you have on others? Our world needs all the bright, shiny, and full-spectrum Technicolor you have to offer. Yes, HD color that lifts people up and spreads joy, hope, and happiness. So bring it. Share it. Adding color matters.

MERE COLOR, UNSPOILED BY MEANING, AND UNALLIED WITH DEFINITE FORM, CAN SPEAK TO THE SOUL IN A THOUSAND DIFFERENT WAYS.

—Oscar Wilde

TAKE ACTION

HIGH: Implement an add-color policy to all meals or meetings this week, where every meal or meeting begins with COLOR. Maybe it is someone sharing a joyful story or everyone sharing something quick, uplifting, or new. See how it changes the energy in the room and your time together.

MEDIUM: Draw a self-portrait and include the colors you imagine are in your aura. Sure, maybe people can't see all of your glorious colors glowing, but how do you show these colors in different ways? In your smile? Through your many acts of kindness? In how you laugh? Keep glowing.

LOW: Paint an interior wall a bright color of your choosing. If actually painting a wall is not an option, then simply add some flowers or a vibrant painting or collage of images to your environment.

THIS WEEK...
LOVE THE LITTLE THINGS

TAKE ACTION

HIGH: Start a little-things art display at your workplace, your child's school, or even on a random fence in your neighborhood that features pictures of little things that bring joy. Keep adding to it over time, and invite others to add pictures as well. Joy walls are good walls.

MEDIUM: Create a little-things calendar by adding one little thing you are going to do each day this week to bring you or others joy. Pick a flower, read an inspirational quote, watch the clouds, or cook a meal. Be a catalyst of joy, one little act at a time.

LOW: Is there a little thing you have been dying to treat yourself to but, for one reason or another, you just haven't? Then today is your day. Do it. When you do, enjoy it to the fullest.

> **THE LITTLE THINGS? THE LITTLE MOMENTS? THEY AREN'T LITTLE.**
>
> —Jon Kabat-Zinn

Even though snow is made up of millions of snowflakes, no two alike, we tend to just see snow. The same goes for sand at the beach. In other words, we tend to mostly notice things in broad strokes, not appreciating the little miracles or events that create the bigger picture. But living this way doesn't allow us to fully thrive and feel all the joy that surrounds us. So this week, let's slow down, take a closer look, and **LOVE THE LITTLE THINGS**. Every day, there are mini-events of awesomeness that take place and easily pass us by. It's someone's shy smile. It's a winter sunset. It's hearing the words *I love you*. These are priceless and timeless moments and truly the stuff that matters most in life. These little moments, strung together day after day, week after week, year after year, make for a joyful life. However, instead of truly soaking these moments in, we complain that time keeps going faster and faster. Well, I promise, if you spend more time connecting to the little joys you get to enjoy every day, your life will slow down and improve dramatically. Loving the little things matters.

MONDAY GETS SELFLESS

There is an adjective that I believe most of us hope others would use to describe us. It might not be the first word they choose, but it would be nice if it made the Top 5 list. The word is *selfless*. Its definition is short, but it says a lot: "To be more concerned with the needs of others than with one's own." The reason I find this word so powerful is because it has a way of combining power players, like compassion, generosity, and kindness all into one little eight-letter package. But just because we might want to be known for our selflessness doesn't mean we have actually earned it. Reputation is a funny thing…and so is legacy. They are both built one moment at a time. No, not starting ten or twenty years from now, either. Starting right this minute, and five minutes from now, and so on. So starting right now, are you ready to earn it? It is often said there are givers and takers in life. Let's make this month all about how much we can give and inspire our friends, family, coworkers, and classmates to do the same. Being selfless matters.

THIS WEEK...
GO SECOND

We live in a competitive world. As they say, there is only one first-place trophy, and second place is really just the first loser. We see competitiveness in schools, workplaces, sports, and yes, even on freeways: "That's my spot." "I deserve that promotion." We are driven by a strong sense of entitlement—that it is "mine, mine, mine." Can't you hear the seagulls in *Finding Nemo* right now? Now, I believe that competition is healthy; it drives us to work harder, push our limits, and grow. The problem is that these benefits are not typically what drives us. Rather, it's our need to win in order to feel good about ourselves or to prove our worth to others that fuels us. So let's recalibrate a little bit and choose to **GO SECOND** this week. That's right, let them have that parking spot and be first in line on Black Friday. And when it comes to accomplishing your goals, do it because it is a personal achievement, not in the spirit of beating someone else. No, this isn't about participation trophies. It's just about trusting that everything is going to be just fine even when they go first. Going second matters.

TO LEAD PEOPLE, WALK BEHIND THEM.

— Anonymous

TAKE ACTION

HIGH: Every time you're waiting in line, about to get on an elevator, or parking in a crowded lot, give someone else the right-of-way. Then notice their reaction when you wave them ahead, and check your own feelings in the moment too. It promises to please.

MEDIUM: Ever cut someone off that was trying to merge into your lane? It's OK, we've all done it. But take a minute to identify situations in your life where your pursuit of being first might seem a bit ridiculous or even unsafe. Then commit to changing the program.

LOW: Get into a little friendly competition for a day or two or even a week. Do it with yourself or a friend. How many times can you intentionally go second, put someone else first, or sacrifice something you want in order to help someone else?

THIS WEEK...
DO WITHOUT

TAKE ACTION

HIGH: Give something every week. Instead of that coffee and muffin every day, donate that breakfast money to a worthy cause. Instead of buying another pair of shoes you don't need, buy a pair for someone who really needs them. You get the drill. Think you can do it? I do.

MEDIUM: What if instead of people giving you a gift for your birthday this year, you asked them to donate money or items to people in need or an organization that serves them. By doing without yourself, you are doing a lot for others.

LOW: Give yourself a goal to clean out your gently used items for a few hours this week, and see how many treasures you can collect and donate to others.

MATERIALISM IS AN IDENTITY CRISIS.

—Bryant H. McGill

Do you own more than thirty pairs of shoes? Have you bought the newest golf driver every year for the past ten years, and now you have ten "old" drivers? Do you struggle with getting rid of stuff because fashion repeats itself or once you lose ten pounds, those pants will fit again? If you can relate to any of this, then this week is just for you. It's time to **DO WITHOUT**. There is a saying that sums this week up perfectly: "If you have it to give, then give it." Well, we all do, and I have proof—public storage in the United States is a twenty-five-billion-dollar industry, currently providing over 2.5 billion square feet of storage space for our stuff. In other words, we have so much stuff that we can't keep it under our own roofs, so we pay someone else to store it for us. I find that troubling. There are people who can use and will appreciate our stuff, so let's give it freely and even save some money on rental fees while we are at it. Let's stop collecting and squeezing so tightly. We can't take it with us anyway. Doing without matters.

CONSPIRE FOR GOOD

Did we really step foot on the moon? Did Jesus marry Mary Magdalene? Are Elvis and Tupac really gone? Oh, how we love a good conspiracy theory. So clandestine. So sinister. So #FakeNews. Well, I have a conspiracy theory to share with you that has been happening every single Monday for years. You are now a willing and active participant in it too. So get ready to **CONSPIRE FOR GOOD**. Yes, there is a secret team of people in the world that wakes up every morning with the passion and goal of serving others. Crazy, right? Well, not according to the research. In fact, volunteering has been proven to lower blood pressure, ward off loneliness, increase self-esteem, and lengthen life expectancy. Now that you know this, you might even recognize someone on this team, because they have what's called a giver's glow. Oh wait, I can hear a new conspiracy theory brewing right now: "Doing good is a selfish act." To this, I say, "Then let's create the most selfish world we have ever seen." Because seven billion people selfishly conspiring for good might be the greatest conspiracy of all time. Welcome to the secret society. Conspiring for good matters.

THE WORLD IS CHANGED BY YOUR EXAMPLE, NOT BY YOUR OPINION.

—Paulo Coelho

TAKE ACTION

HIGH: Plan a give-back event! Connect with a local agency to find out how they can best use your time, talent, and/or treasure. Then make it happen. Trust me, it is going to feel good to do good. So why not make it a regular thing? Keep conspiring for good.

MEDIUM: On your own or with a few friends or family members, make some sack lunches or care kits and get out there and share them with those in need. Use this time to do even more good by talking and really connecting with those you share with as well.

LOW: Find simple ways to serve. Pick up trash as you walk to lunch; clean out the supply closet at work; or thank a veteran, firefighter, or law enforcement officer the next time you see one. The options are endless, but they all matter and fuel our little conspiracy.

SMILE AT A STRANGER

TAKE ACTION

HIGH: We all love lemonade stands. Well, what about a smile booth? Try a booth at your work, school, community park, or even at home. Ask people to step inside the booth to share their smile. See how many smile photos you can get, and share them on social with #smilesmatter.

MEDIUM: Socialize your smile. Post a selfie of your smile on social media and encourage your followers to do the same thing. Zoom in! This isn't about your outfit or where you are; it is all about your smile. Use #smiles-matter and let's get a little viral smile campaign going.

LOW: Commit to smiling throughout the day at everyone and anyone you interact with. Make sure to take note of how people react and how it makes you feel, and, of course, don't be afraid to just smile away even when you're by yourself.

> LET US ALWAYS MEET EACH OTHER WITH A SMILE, FOR THE SMILE IS THE BEGINNING OF LOVE.
>
> —Mother Teresa

You hold a special gift that only you possess. Actually, every-one has this gift, but each is unique. What is it? It's your smile. Maybe you go gums and all. Maybe you just show a little bit of teeth or even have a crooked one. The truth is that just about every smile has a name for it: "The Victory Smile," "The Old Friend Smile," "The Love Smile," "The Reminiscent Smile," and best of all, "The Face Ache." Yes, that's the one that causes your face to hurt because you are laughing so hard. Well, in the spirit of being selfless, it's time to **SMILE AT A STRANGER**. A smile from the right person at the right time can change everything, and when it comes from someone you don't even know, it's just all the more unexpected and awesome. And please don't go to that "Isn't that a little creepy?" place. Because if our culture has come to a place where smiling at one another is creepy, we have some serious work to do. Smiles uplift. They say "I see you." They are even contagious. Yes, just like yawning, smiling begets smiling. So smile early and often. Smiling matters.

MONDAY GETS QUIET

Life gets busy. We have work, school, family, friends, meetings, practices, games, grocery shopping, exercise, bills, and so on. But we can't always blame our busyness on life, for our calendars don't fill themselves out…we do. Driven by a sense of bigger, stronger, faster, we pack more into our schedules than can possibly fit. Then, in a state of surprise, we utter the words, "Wow, I got eight hours of sleep last night, and I still feel tired." Should we really be that shocked, or have we all signed up for the I-guess-I-had-to-get-sick-in-order-to-slow-down program? Even more disturbing: the super healthy I'll-sleep-when-I-am-dead plan. Neither of these programs are working for us. Our minds, hearts, and bodies need to rest, and we need to start intentionally creating space for this to happen. We need to rejuvenate, refill, and pace ourselves. Enough liking likes, enough noise, enough checking off our lists. It's time to step away, turn it off, and slow our roll. I promise you won't miss a beat and that it will be one of the most life-giving and rewarding things you do all year. Getting quiet matters.

THIS WEEK...
UNPLUG

If someone offered you $100 to give up your cell phone for a day, could you do it? Would you do it? What if they offered you $500? Or $1,000? See, most of us freak out when we don't know where our phone is for even a few minutes. It's as if life comes to a complete standstill until we find it, and the universe gets restored. Doesn't something seem wrong here? Remember, it was not long ago that we didn't have cell phones, and we got along just fine. So this week, let's travel back in time in order to **UNPLUG**. I know, this sounds torturous, but isn't that already commentary on how off we are? Sure, there are plenty of pros to having our phones, but our overuse of them has also made us unsafe, rude, disconnected, and distracted. How about these situations—while driving your car, while eating dinner with someone, or while in a movie theater? Fair enough? Our phones have changed us, and it's time to look up and see what we're missing. So this week, choose differently. Be safe. Be present. Be polite. Unplugging matters.

TAKE ACTION

HIGH: Go on a digital diet. No using your cell in the bedroom, only do emails at work, no eating and texting, limit social media to fifteen minutes per day, and please, no texting and driving. Nothing that comes through your phone is worth your or someone else's life.

MEDIUM: The next time you have lunch or dinner with a group, have everyone place their phones on the table, screen-side down, and create a stack in the middle of the table with them. Whoever grabs their phone from the stack to look at it has to pay the bill.

LOW: Sleep and cell phones don't make a good partnership. Leave your phone out of your bedroom. I promise it will be wherever you left it in the morning.

> **ALMOST EVERYTHING WILL WORK AGAIN IF YOU UNPLUG IT FOR A FEW MINUTES, INCLUDING YOU.**
>
> —Anne Lamott

KNOW YOUR EMOTIONS

TAKE ACTION

HIGH: Knowing your emotions starts with sitting quietly and connecting to how you're feeling. Find ten minutes a day to sit quietly. Whatever feelings come up, embrace them, and start there as you reconnect with the world.

MEDIUM: Sometimes it's possible to feel a ton of different emotions at the same time. Sometimes it's also easy to not feel anything at all. If this ever happens to you, choose to focus on gratitude. Even in the worst of times, we all have plenty to be grateful for.

LOW: Find and be an emotional-support buddy. Let the person you pick know that you hope he or she can be there for you and that you're ready to be there for them. Make a pact to not judge as you support one another in the ups and downs in life.

> # EMOTIONS ARE NOT PROBLEMS TO BE SOLVED. THEY ARE SIGNALS TO BE INTERPRETED.
>
> —Vironika Tugaleva

In the early to mid-1600s, French philosopher René Descartes penned the infamous line, "I think, therefore I am." Ever since, we have equated our human existence and the thing that makes the human race so superior to all other life forms with our ability to think. But this ignores a part of us that can no longer hide in the shadows; it is literally killing us. So get ready to **KNOW YOUR EMOTIONS**. We have a societal stigma that is in urgent need of change. It's the idea that feeling too much is a personal problem we must bear alone. That very real feelings like anxiety, depression, fear, hopelessness, and despair are not to be talked about at the dinner table and are only for the sick. But this thought process couldn't be further from where we should be as a society. We share responsibility for our emotional health. It's time for all of us to start being really honest with ourselves and with those we love when it comes to our feelings. No more judgment. No more fear of sharing. Only acceptance, love, and support. So get ready to dig in and feel deeply. Knowing your emotions matters.

GET OUTDOORS

There is something we do over twenty thousand times a day and don't even think about. Wherever we are and whatever we do, it happens. It's called *breathing*. But shouldn't something that we do this often and can't live without get a little more of our attention? I think it should. And without getting too scientific, I want to specifically propose the breathing of outdoor air, not that indoor stuff circulating through the vents. So get ready to **GET OUTDOORS**. On average, we spend 93 percent of our lives indoors. That means that only 7 percent of our lives are spent outdoors. I would imagine that the majority of that 7 percent isn't even spent in the kind of outdoors that I am talking about here. Yes, walking down a busy sidewalk in the middle of a city is certainly outdoors, but this isn't serving us either. Think "outdoors" outdoors, like in nature. Away from it all. Where we can get quiet, see the wonder of nature, listen to the birds, and smell the grass, trees, and flowers. This is where life-giving breath happens, and this is what we need more of...starting today. Getting outdoors matters.

> **LOOK DEEP INTO NATURE, AND THEN YOU WILL UNDERSTAND EVERYTHING BETTER.**
>
> —Anonymous

TAKE ACTION

HIGH: Start a walking group that commits to walking at least three times a week. Join a softball, beach volleyball, soccer, or any other outdoor sports league. Create a hiking group, and take on a new trail every week. It's a win-win.

MEDIUM: Think of something you do consistently every day that typically happens indoors. Then start to replace one of your typical indoor habits with an outdoor one. Hint: find a good nearby park. You can eat, read, and exercise there.

LOW: Find five minutes a day to sit quietly outside without looking at your cell phone. Instead, revel in the nature you can see, hear, and smell.

47

SAY NO TO SAY YES

TAKE ACTION

HIGH: Is there a routine in your life that hasn't necessarily been working for you? Well, it's time for some new boundaries. Communicate the changes with love but also with a strong message that says, "I have to say no to say yes to myself."

MEDIUM: Have a meeting of the minds with your coworkers, family members, or fellow volunteers. Present the problem you're experiencing with being the go-to person on all that you're handling. Then ask the team to offer ideas for how that workload can be more evenly distributed.

LOW: Pick one thing this week that you would typically say yes to and choose to say no instead. It's OK—really.

> IF YOUR COMPASSION DOES NOT INCLUDE YOURSELF, IT IS INCOMPLETE.
>
> —Jack Kornfield

We are people pleasers. We own this title to varying degrees, but it's in all of us. Why? Because we care what people think about us, and we hope that people like us. Because of this, we have become really good at saying yes. We say yes to our friends, our kids, our company, and everyone else's priorities and schedules. The problem is that with all these yeses, we end up saying no to ourselves. But this week, we are going to **SAY NO TO SAY YES**. This means we need to start saying no to something in our lives in order to create time and space to say yes to ourselves. This idea might conjure up thoughts like "Wow, this kind of sounds rude" or "Wow, this sounds amazing." I promise there is nothing rude about this. You matter too, and your needs are equally as important. Remember, no one can serve from an empty bowl, so filling up our own bowls needs to be a priority as well. In the end, everyone wins, because we feel better and we have more to give. Saying no to say yes matters.

MONDAY GETS HUMAN

We are humans. Scientifically classified as *Homo sapiens*, which in Latin translates to "wise man," or in our time, "wise person." Sounds good, right? Well, just because we are all *Homo sapiens* doesn't seem to make us automatically so wise. It also doesn't paint the fullest picture of what it means to be human. What about our ability to feel? To connect and communicate? To create and invent? To intuitively know right from wrong and to share a dream for a world that promotes common good? See, this is all part of being human and the part of each one of us that I want to dive into this month. Why? Because there are endless opportunities to be *better* at being human. We can express ourselves better. We can use kinder words and take more caring actions. We can be better friends and parents. We can even be better strangers to one another. Let's explore and engage in what it truly means to be human with the goal of being the best human beings possible. Embracing our humanness and humanity matters.

THIS WEEK...
TAKE THE HIGH ROAD

As humans, we often think being right is more important than being kind. It is almost like we see being kind as losing and being right as winning. But what does that really get us? The answer is *nothing*. Well, maybe it gets us some sort of personal satisfaction and feeds our ego a little bit, but is that really winning us anything? In fact, maybe we have it completely backward, and being kind is actually what it truly means to win. So this week, we are going to win by choosing to **TAKE THE HIGH ROAD**. Every day, we are presented with situations that cause us to make little and big character decisions. Sometimes they include another person, and other times we have to make these decisions when we are alone and no one is watching. These moments in life test our moral compass. Do we choose the right thing, even though it might not be the easiest thing? Do we just walk away or try to work it out? Do we leave a note on the car with our name and phone number? The kind road is the winning road. Taking the high road matters.

THE HIGH ROAD IS ALWAYS RESPECTED. HONESTY AND INTEGRITY ARE ALWAYS REWARDED.

—Scott Hamilton

TAKE ACTION

HIGH: Discuss with your coworkers how you can take the high road when dealing with challenging customers or each other. Post a list of high-road strategies to help everyone remember how easy it is to win when we take the high road. Adapt this for your family and friends.

MEDIUM: Pick someone you may have taken the low or more selfish road with recently and reach out to make amends. Offer an apology. Genuinely offer to try to look at things from their perspective going forward.

LOW: Add a high-road Post-it Note to your computer monitor, office area, or somewhere at home. Let it work as a helpful reminder to choose kindness by taking the high road today, every day, and forever.

PRIORITIZE PEOPLE

TAKE ACTION

HIGH: Consider how everyone you know could get involved in helping a group of people in your community. Then invite them to put aside their own priorities for a little while to make others a priority. Who knows? Maybe this can become a lasting people-first priority habit.

MEDIUM: Make a list of the most important people in your life. Then list the things you could do that you know would mean the world to them. Then work through the list one person and one action at a time.

LOW: Are you the person always turning others down on getting together? Well, stop it. Say yes to putting the people in your life first. Accept their invitations, do something spontaneous with your loved ones, or just pick up the phone and call someone.

> **NOBODY CARES HOW MUCH YOU KNOW UNTIL THEY KNOW HOW MUCH YOU CARE.**
>
> —Anonymous

Priorities are everywhere. Companies develop them as a way to drive success. Schools have them to help their students succeed. Political parties have them to win voters and to set their agendas. We each have them too. Some are clear in our minds, like our New Year's resolutions—lose weight, make more money, or quit a bad habit—while others are more unspoken, simply interwoven into our daily decisions and actions. Our priorities keep us focused and progressing those important things in our lives. But how often do we make people a priority? How many times do we prioritize our loved ones, friends, colleagues, neighbors, or those in need? Well, it's time to **PRIORITIZE PEOPLE**. Think about someone in your life for a moment. Maybe it's a best friend, parent, spouse, or coworker. Then ask yourself, "What is one thing I can do this week to show that person how much they mean to me?" Once you have your answer, the only thing left to do is to do it. It's that easy. Let's park our own wants and needs for a bit and instead focus on someone near and dear to us. Prioritizing people matters.

FORGIVE FREELY

If you are someone who has never made a mistake or never hurt anyone's feelings, then you can skip this Monday...and please share your secrets for success! However, if you are like most members of this big club called human beings, then please keep reading. We are not proud of it, but the truth is that we have all been hurt by and have hurt someone. But what happened afterward, I might argue, could be more important than the initial hurt. It's called *forgiveness*. Ah... the *F* word. I know, it's not easy. Well, no one ever said being human was easy, and this week is no exception. Let's **FORGIVE FREELY**. Forgiveness can be a double standard. We want people to forgive us, yet we have a difficult time forgiving others. Well, life doesn't work that way. We should never expect to be forgiven if we can't forgive. So who do you need to forgive? Maybe it is something someone did recently. Or maybe it was something that happened five, ten, or even fifteen years ago. It's time to stop carrying that stuff around; it only weighs us down. Forgiveness leads to freedom. Forgiving freely matters.

IT'S ONE OF THE GREATEST GIFTS YOU CAN GIVE YOURSELF, TO FORGIVE. FORGIVE EVERYBODY.

—Maya Angelou

TAKE ACTION

HIGH: Take on your toughest forgiveness challenge. Face the person (dead or alive) who you want or need to forgive. Before you go there, prepare mentally by reliving that moment and truly connecting to your humanity, love, and faith. Then let it go with the three simple words "I forgive you."

MEDIUM: Spend time each day reflecting on the areas in your life where you may need to show yourself greater kindness and acceptance. We all are pretty good at being self-critical, beating ourselves up, and not forgiving ourselves. Enough already. Give yourself some grace. You deserve it.

LOW: Start small. What are some simple things that happen throughout your day that really tick you off? Maybe when someone cuts you off in traffic? Maybe when someone interrupts you? Well, do your best to shrug it off. It's good practice for you.

57

PRACTICE PATIENCE

TAKE ACTION

HIGH: Write a note of apology or reach out to someone you may have lost your patience with recently. Maybe it was that new teller at your bank who slowed you down or the restaurant waiter who kept forgetting your iced tea. Hint: Gift cards always do wonders.

MEDIUM: Tune in to your patience barometer this week. When you start to feel yourself losing your patience, try dialing it back and reading yourself. After all, being tired and hungry never seems to help our patience levels. The smallest change can make a surprising and very calming difference.

LOW: Practice patience with yourself. Find a word or phrase that you can say, such as "chill" or "let go," when you find yourself in a situation that tests your patience. Enjoy your new personal patience mantra. Use it as often as you need to. Remember, patience starts and ends with you.

ADOPT THE PACE OF NATURE. HER SECRET IS PATIENCE.

—Ralph Waldo Emerson

Foot tappers. Watch watchers. Barista starers. Horn honkers. Tailgaters. This week is just for you. But I just need a few more minutes of your precious time to give some context. Because this is an important week...like, really important. It is something that can benefit all of us, and it can't be rushed or forced. It's going to take a minute, so let's just breathe and feel our way through this. I know it's not easy. It might actually cause us to think we're losing our minds, and we might feel that rush of blood to our faces, the crawl of the hair on the backs of our necks, or the roll of our eyes. You there yet? You ready to skip to next Monday? Good, because now you're really in touch with why this week, you get to **PRACTICE PATIENCE**. This was just a small test for you. But don't worry, there are lots more of those practice tests ahead, because this is just part of living in this great big, wonderful, human-filled world. So stop tapping, watching, staring, and honking. There's a reason for the saying "Patience is a virtue." Practicing patience matters.

MONDAY GETS CREATIVE

You are one of a kind. Of the over seven billion people on earth right now, not one single person is the same as you. They don't look the same, think the same, sound the same, feel the same. This means that you matter, because there is only one YOU. It also reminds us that we live in a very creative and diverse world, because the same rule applies to animals, flowers, trees, clouds, etc. Everything is unique. But how much time do we spend thinking about how this plays out in our creativity? Do we take enough time to appreciate our personal and very individual creativity and the creativity all around us? Better yet, do we spend enough time being creative, both on our own and collectively? There is something very powerful and ironic about creativity—it allows us all to be so different, yet it is also the very thing that connects us. Isn't that what music does? Isn't that what the ancient artifacts do? Isn't that what imagination offers us? So get ready to unleash your creative genius. You were created to create. Being creative matters.

BE IN ART AWE

Art is one of the universe's greatest gifts. It is through art that we are able to experience someone else's world; learn about past civilizations; and express, cherish, and celebrate life's natural and human-made creativity. But I am not convinced we take enough time to appreciate or partake in art, so this week let's **BE IN ART AWE**. Now, I can already hear the left side of your brain saying, "This is so illogical. I am not an artist." But as the spokesperson for the right side of your brain, I am here to tell you—and the left side of your brain— that you are an artist. In fact, everyone is an artist in their own special way. It's just a matter of connecting to something you love doing. Do you like to cook? Then you're an artist. Do you doodle? Then you're an artist. Are you a good friend? Then you're an artist. See, there is really no excuse to not connect with art this week. Have fun and be forgiving with it, because there is no such thing as perfection. Whatever you create is absolutely perfect...because you created it. Let your inner artist shine. Art matters.

TAKE ACTION

HIGH: Replicate a piece from one of your favorite artists. Paint a Picasso or sculpt your own David. Or maybe you are a thespian and want to take your talents to the stage or in front of a camera. YouTube is ready for your upload.

MEDIUM: Did you use to express yourself creatively a lot more than you do now? Miss it? Then bring it back. Ceramics, doodling, woodworking, gardening, cooking, acting, story writing, dancing, guitar playing…they all qualify. Go for it and even consider inviting friends to join you.

LOW: Seek out some form of artistic expression that inspires you. Take a walk in a sculpture garden, enjoy a live performance, visit a museum, eat something gourmet, or watch a sunset from start to finish. Start to open your mind and warm up that right side of your brain.

> **THE PURPOSE OF ART IS WASHING THE DUST OF DAILY LIFE OFF OUR SOULS.**
>
> —Anonymous

BUILD SOMETHING

TAKE ACTION

HIGH: Already pretty handy and creative? Then it's time to go bigger. Maybe a neighborhood fence could use some love. Or maybe it's time to build a picnic table and benches for your backyard or a local community garden. Bring friends along to share your joy and expertise for building stuff.

MEDIUM: Think about something you have always wanted in your home. Find some tutorials, buy the supplies, and give it a shot. Just remember to measure twice and cut once, not the other way around. And please don't forget to celebrate a job well done.

LOW: Starting from scratch can be a little more challenging, so do some research and order a pre-made kit to make a little something special for someone you love. Whether it's a jewelry box for your mom or a new dog house for your furry friend, building and giving go hand-in-hand.

> # PREDICTING RAIN DOESN'T COUNT. BUILDING ARKS DOES.
>
> —Warren Buffett

Our hands are incredible creations. Each of our hands has twenty-seven bones in it. Pretty remarkable, considering our arms only have three bones. And somehow, these twenty-seven bones are connected and work together to do amazing feats. We can use them to communicate, to grab, to make sounds, and to feel emotions. Yet for many of us, we have relegated our hands to something very limiting. It's called typing "FJFJFJFJ" and texting "LOL, OMG, BRB." So in the spirit of honoring the fifty-four bones in our two hands and all of the awesomeness they can perform, it's time to **BUILD SOMETHING**. Ever watch one of the many home remodeling or redecorating shows on television and say to yourself, "Wow, that is beautiful. I wish my house looked like that"? Well, give it a shot. Look around your house and think of something like a bench, a picture frame, or a table, and see if you can build your own. If this seems a little daunting, then get those hands dirty and plant something in your garden. Here are just a few handy tips for you: start small, be safe, protect your precious hands, and have fun. Building something matters.

SURPRISE THE WORLD

Without creativity, there is no art. In other words, there wouldn't be songs, paintings, photographs, movies, or dance without creativity. There also wouldn't be cars, cell phones, toothbrushes, or any other invention for that matter. After all, these all began as creative ideas and exist today as tangible expressions of those ideas. Well, there is another art form that doesn't get included on most lists of most popular art forms—the art of the surprise. So this week, get ready to **SURPRISE THE WORLD**. When was the last time someone surprised you or you surprised someone else? Maybe it was a simple love note in the sock drawer or buying coffee for the person behind you in line. Or maybe it was something more elaborate, like decorating someone's office or shocking someone with concert tickets on the day of the show. See, you are already starting to smile just thinking about those little sneaky, creative acts of joy. Well, it's time to unleash more of them. Go put some smiles on people's faces...and good luck keeping a straight face while you are at it. Surprises matter, because they let people know how much they matter.

THOSE WHO ARE EASILY SHOCKED SHOULD BE SHOCKED MORE OFTEN.

— Mae West

TAKE ACTION

HIGH: Plan a surprise for someone that includes others. These surprises require more organization and a lot of trust in the people you include, but they can also be the most rewarding. Just remember that whatever you do you should only surprise and not shock the person you have in mind.

MEDIUM: Plan one super personal surprise for a special person you might be taking for granted. Don't overthink it. Just go with your gut and make it a genuine expression of caring.

LOW: Think of three people you would like to surprise with something quick and simple. Maybe it is a Post-it Note they will surely see, a long-overdue phone call, or a special delivery. Keep it simple, but just know how much they are going to love and appreciate it.

THIS WEEK...
ENJOY VARIETY

TAKE ACTION

HIGH: Organize an international potluck and invite your friends, colleagues, and family members. Have everyone bring and present their favorite home-cooked dishes from around the world. Oh, and don't forget to set up a great international playlist before everyone arrives. Share all the recipes after the party wraps!

MEDIUM: Use the internet to do a little research on adding variety to your life. Find new local international-inspired eateries, upcoming concerts, dance performances, or exhibits featuring cultures you aren't familiar with. Variety is the spice of life. So get out there and add some spice.

LOW: Do you always eat the same things for breakfast, lunch, and dinner? Then replace your usual with some new menu items. Same goes for your fashion, your typical route to work, and what you do for exercise. Change it all up. It's fun.

THE ESSENCE OF THE BEAUTIFUL IS UNITY IN VARIETY.

—Moses Mendelssohn

Imagine walking into a restaurant and the menu simply said: Drink. Salad. Fish. Soup. Sandwich. Dessert. Why just one word? Because there is only one option. You want a sandwich, then order the sandwich. Same goes for the salad. When you look at the tables around you, you see people eating the exact same sandwich you are. What's even stranger is those other people also look and dress just like you. Then, as you are driving home to your house that looks just like everyone else's, you notice that everyone is driving the exact same car as you. Why? Because there is only one car. OK, I will stop now, because this is getting painful. Instead, let's **ENJOY VARIETY**. Variety is one of the greatest gifts of having so many unique and beautiful cultures in our world. No matter where we live, we can experience the music, food, clothing, and art from around the world. But how much variety do we truly enjoy, or are we just creatures of habit? In the spirit of being creative, let's embrace all of the creative options around us. Think of it as a little adventure. Enjoying variety matters.

MONDAY GETS CONNECTED

I'm not sure whether Fred McFeely Rogers knew how disconnected our culture would become, but 895 times, from 1968–2001, Mr. Rogers came onto our television screens and asked us to be his neighbor. Today, many of us don't even know our neighbors' names, let alone anything else about them. So much for borrowing milk or butter. Now we can just have it delivered. Heaven forbid we actually need to leave our homes. We simply hop in our cars in the garage, press the Open button on our garage door controller, and off we go. When we get home, we hit the Open button before we even hit our driveways, simply to pull into our garage, shut the door, and go back inside. Not a neighbor seen or a word shared. Sure, we have our hundreds of social media "friends," but we are quickly realizing that these aren't friends at all. Today, we are left with a culture that is disconnected, lonely, and wondering why we feel like something is missing. Well, there is something missing—relationships, connections, belonging—and only we can fix it. This month, get ready to leave your private island of one. Connecting matters.

CONNECT TO COMMUNITY

Have you ever thought about the fact that we all live on a giant rock that spins at the rate of 1,000 miles per hour as it travels 584 million miles per year around another even bigger object? As all of this is happening, we have each staked out our little plot of land on this giant spinning rock and called it *home*. As our little plots of land started to bump up to one another, we started to build what we call villages, towns, and cities. In other words, we formed communities because of our geographical proximity. But just because we live close to one another doesn't necessarily mean we act much like a community—a connected group of people. So this week is all about **CONNECTING TO COMMUNITY**, because that's what neighborly neighbors do. In order for communities to thrive, every single individual within them must embrace their role. See, communities aren't over there somewhere and we are over here. No, we are the community; without the collective *we,* there is no community. So let's plug into it even more. Interact. Celebrate. Relate. Grow. Connecting to community matters.

IN EVERY COMMUNITY,
THERE IS WORK
TO BE DONE. IN EVERY
NATION, THERE ARE
WOUNDS TO HEAL.
IN EVERY HEART,
THERE IS THE POWER
TO DO IT.

— Marianne Williamson

TAKE ACTION

HIGH: Create a community-connection team, and commit to exploring something new in your community once a month. Check out a concert in the park, farmers' market, or a new museum. See how many new community friends you can make along the way and grow the team. Mr. Rogers would be proud.

MEDIUM: Meet five new people in your community. Maybe it is your mailperson, your waiter or waitress, a new coworker, the principal at your children's school, or even your neighbor.

LOW: Do some research on your city. Learn its history; check out the scene; find local classes, flavors, and volunteer opportunities. You might be surprised by how much it has to offer and how actively involved people already are. They are just waiting to meet you, so get out there.

GET A GROUP

TAKE ACTION

HIGH: Do you have a hobby or something new you want to explore? Research a group to join and join it. You would be surprised by how many people out there share your same interests. Have fun and make some new friends while you're at it.

MEDIUM: Identify the different groups you are involved in. Maybe there is a work group, friend group, hip-hop class, or book club. Then assess how actively engaged (or not) you are in each of them, and set a goal to engage more with the ones that really float your boat.

LOW: Take some time to be honest with yourself and consider what holds you back or keeps you from being a part of a group. Why are you lacking that connection? Is it a time thing? Fear? Find your reason, then push through it. You have friends waiting to meet you.

WITH TRUE FRIENDS... EVEN WATER DRUNK TOGETHER IS SWEET ENOUGH.

—African proverb

Human beings are social creatures who thrive off relationships, connectedness, and community. Yes, even you social introverts. The problem is that we don't do a very good job of actually living this way. We spend more time living inside our own heads than being present with one another. To make matters worse, we've convinced ourselves that having friends, fans, or followers on social media is synonymous with having true relationships. Well, it's not…and we are seeing the negative effects of it every day. So this week, it's time for all of us to get a grip and **GET A GROUP**. Isolation and loneliness are devastating to our health. Some even argue that they are more deadly than obesity. Yet instead of actively connecting with one another, we find ourselves saying things like "I wish I had more friends," "I wish I knew people who had the same interests as me," or "I wish someone understood me." The most confusing part is that we are all sitting around saying the same things instead of actually connecting with one another. So stop wishing and starting doing. Join one or start one—getting a group matters.

THIS WEEK...
FIND COMMON GROUND

Labels are a simple yet powerful system we use for organizing information. We use them to delineate months of the year, to categorize types of art, and even to specify how we like our coffee. But as necessary and efficient as labels may be, they can also have a negative effect on the world. Why? Because labels cause us to focus too much on our differences—white, black, brown, Republican, Independent, Democrat, woman, man, kid, adult—instead of what we have in common. Maybe instead of thinking of labels that emphasize our differences, we can strive to use labels that describe what we have in common—humans, animal lovers, dreamers, and friends. This week, we are going to push our differences aside to **FIND COMMON GROUND**, because as different as we all might be, we have just as much, if not more, in common. At our core, we all have the same needs and desires—shelter, food, water, love, relationships, purpose, and happiness. We also share the same hope for a kind, supportive, healthy, and safe world. So let's come together under the label of "World Changers" to see what we can accomplish. Finding common ground matters.

TAKE ACTION

HIGH: Gather a group of friends, family, or coworkers, and ask everyone to offer one label that is causing issues in your community today. Maybe it has to do with race, religion, sex, age, or politics. As a group, discuss how these labels can be turned into something positive and constructive.

MEDIUM: Think of five labels that you use for people and what meanings you attach to them. Then challenge yourself to replace these potentially negative labels with new, positive ones based on similarities instead of differences.

LOW: Ask yourself how you typically respond to disagreements or conflicts? Do you tend to dig in and keep the conflict going, or are you one of the first to work toward common ground? If you are the stubborn type, challenge yourself to move more toward being a common-ground finder.

> # WE BUILD TOO MANY WALLS AND NOT ENOUGH BRIDGES.
>
> —Joseph Fort

THIS WEEK...
MAKE THE FIRST MOVE

TAKE ACTION

HIGH: Has a new family moved onto your street? Did a new employee just start at your place of work? Consider yourself the make-the-first-move welcoming committee. No doubt they will appreciate it, and you just might make a new friend.

MEDIUM: Make the first move with every person you interact with this week, even if others seem surprised. Studies have proven that the majority of people in elevators either stare at the numbers above the door or at their feet. So hearing you say "Hi" might throw them for a loop.

LOW: Making the first move might sound a bit scary, so start simply. Think of what works for you. Maybe it's a simple nod or smile. If that's your starting point, then that is the perfect plan. We just need to start somewhere and build from there.

> **CONVERSATION IS FOOD FOR THE SOUL.**
>
> —Mexican proverb

Imagine entering an elevator and three other people are already inside. Imagine standing in line at the grocery store with someone in front and in back of you. Now, imagine what you typically do in these situations. Do you say anything? Do anything? Or do you simply do your best to ignore the other people, avoiding eye contact and conversation at all cost? I have a hunch on how you might have answered those questions, so this week, it's time to **MAKE THE FIRST MOVE**. How is it possible that we have created a culture where it is easier to ignore one another than it is to engage in the simplest of friendly gestures? Eye contact. A smile. A nod. Dare we even utter the word *hello*? Don't these actions seem easy enough and more natural to take than dodging one another? Maybe I am a little bit old-school, but when did ignoring someone become not rude? Connecting and communicating go hand-in-hand. Staring at our cell phone screens is just a big face-to-face-interaction, make-a-connection, make-the-first-move sucker. So look up and connect. It takes just two seconds, but it speaks volumes. Making the first move matters.

MONDAY GETS AWARE

We live in a dynamic world. Things are moving faster than ever. Exposure to anything and everything is delivered right to us in the palms of our hands. Not only can it be overwhelming, but it can also create so much noise and such a blur that connecting to any of it seems impossible. In fact, sometimes it just feels like a whole lot of ants on a page, and nothing really jumps out anymore. However, when we stop for a moment and pull back, even just one layer, we begin to see how important each and every event or experience really is. We can see ourselves in the middle of the chaos and ask ourselves so many of those important self questions, like *Who am I?* or *What is my role in all this?* As we look closer, we can see other people and begin to consider who they are and wonder about their experiences. The next thing we realize is that we are all an equal part of this dynamic and ever-changing fabric of humanity—that is, as long as we are paying attention. Being aware matters.

THIS WEEK...
SEEK EQUALITY

It is really easy for us to think about what we want for ourselves, but how often do we genuinely think about the hopes and dreams of others? Well, we should, because we are all equally deserving of whatever makes our hearts sing, as long as it's not at the cost of someone else's happiness or life. But sometimes we lose sight of this, and we operate from a place of competitiveness, entitlement, or scarcity, as if life is a zero-sum game—if someone gets, then someone doesn't. This only feeds the worst part of us, so from this point forward, let's **SEEK EQUALITY**. If asked, most people would say that everyone deserves the right to food, clean water, shelter, love, health, safety, freedom, and education. Well, it's good that we feel this way, but the truth is that millions of people don't have any of these, and it's not because there isn't enough of it. It's time for all of us to take action against every single injustice and inequality that exists today. Let's be the great equalizers. When I say, "We matter," it means all of us matter. It's a global thing. Seeking equality matters.

IN THE END, WE WILL REMEMBER NOT THE WORDS OF OUR ENEMIES, BUT THE SILENCE OF OUR FRIENDS.

—Martin Luther King Jr.

TAKE ACTION

HIGH: Have you noticed inequality or injustice in your community or even in your workplace? Someone needs you to get involved…and so does the world. Observe, listen, learn, explore options, and then go for it.

MEDIUM: As a family, group of friends, or team of coworkers, pick a global cause to support on an ongoing basis. This is not just a one-and-done thing. Instead make a long-term commitment. When enough of us do our part, we truly can and will make a difference.

LOW: Have you ever experienced feeling not worthy, not respected, not good enough, or not equal in the smallest or biggest of ways? Then you know how it feels. Let this feeling fuel you to get involved so no one else has to ever feel that way. Every single life matters.

OWN IT

TAKE ACTION

HIGH: Take ownership for making your life better. Are you playing the victim? Ignoring the truth? Step it up. If it helps, write a self-improvement contract with yourself that outlines how you're going to tackle this thing once and for all. Include the *whos*, *whats*, and by *whens*, then sign it.

MEDIUM: Create an "own it" group with your coworkers, friends, or family. Maybe it's paying your bills on time, cleaning your room, or calling people back. Help one another own it, then be there to encourage one another to make the necessary changes. We are stronger together.

LOW: In every interaction, take ownership for being kind, doing the right thing, sticking up for others, and making things better. Simply make *taking ownership for a better world* a lifestyle choice.

> THE MOMENT YOU ARE OLD ENOUGH TO TAKE THE WHEEL, RESPONSIBILITY LIES WITH YOU.
>
> —J. K. Rowling

The blame game is one of the worst games ever created. We see it around us every single day in our personal lives and in our larger institutions. As convenient as it might seem, it is not a healthy place from which to operate. At some point, we have to take responsibility for our actions, both individually and collectively. So this week, get ready to **OWN IT**. The first step toward taking ownership is the understanding that no one is perfect. We all make mistakes. This can be difficult for some of us to admit, but it's true. So just embrace it.

Step two is a little more involved. Much like we have for our presidents, imagine we had a civilian approval rating. What would your platform be for improving your community and the lives of people around you? How would you get rated? See, when we stop looking outward, we become more aware of our own *performance* in life, because each one of us is the *what* and the *why*. So let's take responsibility, even when we drop the ball. It's the only way we grow, and it's the only way to live. Owning it matters.

KNOW YOUR ROOTS

Most of us live with a day-by-day lens on life. Twenty-four hours at a time, we create the stories of our lives. But how much time do we spend thinking about the stories of those who preceded us? Their stories are the ones we have unknowingly become the next chapter of, yet we do not always take enough time to fully appreciate or truly know them. Well, it's time to **KNOW YOUR ROOTS**. Your story started long before you were born. It started with your mother's and father's stories, and their parents' stories, and their parents' stories, and all the family stories before them. It probably started in another city, state, or even country. See, the stories that came before you are what make you who you are today. They provide context and understanding of your own behaviors, feelings, and thoughts. It's time for us to start appreciating our larger story in the world. It's time to learn more about the web of circumstances that created us, because learning the interconnectedness of our stories and our roots allows us to see beyond ourselves and broadens our perspectives. Learning your roots matters.

TAKE ACTION

HIGH: Organize a group to visit an elderly home. Our elderly population often feels isolated and depressed, yet they have so much to offer. So go make them feel like they matter!

MEDIUM: Treat someone to lunch and ask them about their family history. It might be something they have not spent much time getting to know, so this will inspire them to discover more about their roots themselves!

LOW: Pick someone in your family—mom, dad, aunt, uncle, grandmother, grandfather, cousin—and ask them about their life. It might just be a brief phone call, but it is one you will be glad you made.

EVERY MAN IS A QUOTATION FROM ALL HIS ANCESTORS.

—Ralph Waldo Emerson

TRACK YOUR TIME

TAKE ACTION

HIGH: Your time is the greatest gift you can give. It's the ultimate gesture of love. Choose whom you want to gift some time to and how you are going to do it. Cherish the special moments ahead.

MEDIUM: Establish a new weekly routine when you block out a chunk of time for yourself. You know your schedule. Once you've set aside the time, (1) do something amazing with it, and (2) protect that block of time with your life. It is yours, and you deserve it.

LOW: Cut back your screen time at least one hour per day. Statistically speaking (so if you're like most of us), that will still leave you forty-three hours of screen time this week, but it will also give you seven newfound hours to do whatever else you want!

TIME IS LONG, BUT LIFE IS SHORT.

—Stevie Wonder

Have you ever had one of those "Where in the heck did the time go?" moments? I would guess you have. Well, the reality is that we can answer this question, if we dare take the time to do so. But I want to warn you, you might not be happy with what you learn. It's time to **TRACK YOUR TIME**. We get 168 hours per week. No one gets more. For most of us, work or school takes up at least forty of those hours, sleep another forty-nine of them. Add three hours a day for eating, bathing, dressing, doing chores, and there goes another twenty-one hours. That leaves…drumroll please…fifty-eight hours per week to do anything else we want or need to do. Well, if you are like the average person, you spend fifty of those hours looking at media for entertainment. That's correct, our free time has become screen time. That means we are not volunteering, exercising, traveling, reading, or spending enough quality time with family or friends. *Ouch*, I know. Well, personal growth starts with awareness, so now we know. Our time is not limitless, so let's start using it wisely. Tracking your time matters.

MONDAY GETS POSITIVE

In many ways, we are pretty simple creatures. We have habits, both good and bad. We like routines, often driving the same roads and ordering the same meals. We also like clarity, black and white, no gray areas. For every up, we have a down. For every on, we have an off. For every cold, we have a hot. It is dualistic. One or the other. Simple. Well, this is the same for *positive* and *negative*. While up or down or hot or cold are harmless and a bit "to each their own," positive and negative pack a bit more of a punch. If I am positive about anything, it's that positivity is more constructive, inspiring, and valuable than negativity. I also believe that our world has plenty of negativity in it already. There is too much judgment, divisiveness, bullying, one-upping, and putting down. But we can change this. So what will you do to make yourself and the world more positive? Let's rediscover how easy it is to be positive with everyone in our lives—friends and strangers alike—and even ourselves. Let's be a true force of positivity. After all, where there is positivity, negativity can't exist. Just ask darkness about light. Being positive matters.

FLIP THE SCRIPT

We all have *that* person in our lives—the one with the half-empty glass. They can't help but see the outcome as turning out poorly. They seem to lack any hope for anything exciting or good. Not even miracles have a shot with these folks. Know who I'm talking about? Have you ever considered whether you have a tendency to be that person? Maybe not all the time, but just now and then? Don't worry if your answer is yes, and don't get down on yourself. Rather, just be ready this week to **FLIP THE SCRIPT**. Boats weren't invented by only focusing on things sinking. Planets aren't explored by assuming we can never reach them. The same goes for our lives and our world. We will only create what we hope for with our positivity turned to the On position. Let's be inspired and focus on the good. Let's believe in a better social ethos that everyone can strive for. Better yet, let's create it together. Because when we change our thoughts on the inside, we change our words and actions on the outside. Flipping the script matters.

IT TAKES NO MORE TIME TO SEE THE GOOD SIDE OF LIFE THAN TO SEE THE BAD.

—Jimmy Buffett

TAKE ACTION

HIGH: Got a pity party going on with your friends, coworkers, or at home? Lead the team in a conversation to call out how the negatives have taken over and that it's time for a change. It takes everyone's agreement to create a culture of positivity.

MEDIUM: Take time to reflect on where you're a negative force and could instead be a positive one. You might be surprised about just how subtly the negativity can show itself. This doesn't mean you are a bad person. It just means it's time to flip your script. Done.

LOW: Imagine a buzzer has just been installed in your brain. Whenever you catch yourself being a naysayer, imagine that little buzzer going off, and immediately change your thoughts, feelings, and words. It's that easy.

ASK "WHY NOT?"

TAKE ACTION

HIGH: Host a "Why not?" gathering for friends and have everyone share a dream or a goal they've always wanted to accomplish. After each person shares their dream, start asking "Why not?" By the end of the gathering, everyone should be out of excuses and ready to take on their goals.

MEDIUM: What's feeling beyond your reach? Maybe it is something at home or work or a personal goal of yours. Turn it into a "Why not?" question, and go for it. You just might find that it is a lot closer to becoming a reality than you realized.

LOW: State something you wish could happen and turn it into a "Why not?" question. For example: "I wish everyone had enough food to eat," becomes "Why not end hunger?" Then answer your question with a way you can help. For example, buy extra food and donate it weekly. Why not?

> YOU SEE THINGS; AND YOU SAY "WHY?" BUT I DREAM THINGS THAT NEVER WERE; AND I SAY, "WHY NOT?"
>
> — George Bernard Shaw

We all have our good friend Socrates to thank for something. It's the question "Why?" We call it the Socratic method, which has been the foundation for all logic and philosophy in the Western world for the last twenty-five hundred years. Well, it's time to introduce Socrates to a new friend. Her name is *Hope*, and she has a new question to ask. This week, Hope wants us to **ASK "WHY NOT?"** Isn't there something about "Why not?" that says "Watch me" or "Don't limit me" or "It's possible"? What if we all asked ourselves—and the world—these questions: "Why not take better care of our health? Why not show one another more love and kindness? Why not shoot for the stars?" See, answering "Why not?" is actually harder than answering the question of "Why?" Don't believe me? Try asking someone one of those three questions, and see if they can give you a good reason not to do what you are asking. Then, why not make every question a "Why not?" question and see how it starts to change your life. Why? Because there isn't anything you can't accomplish. Asking "Why not?" matters.

HARNESS HOPE

We have all heard the saying "When all else fails, there is still hope." In this sense, hope is that final something to hold on to, the last straw. But I tend to see things a bit differently. I see hope as the first thing, where all life and inspiration begin. We hope for more peace in the world. We hope for more happiness. Then we create plans and take steps toward achieving that peace, happiness, or whatever it is that we hope for. But it starts with hope—that feeling of excitement, progress, and belief in what's possible. Can you feel it? Good, because this week, we are all going to **HARNESS HOPE**. What is it that you hope for, and how does hope work for you in your life? Does it lift you up, and is it that anchor in your life that reminds you that every day is a new day to create whatever life you hope to live? If not, is it fair to consider that this might be part of what's holding you back? Either way, let's bring more hope into our lives and the world, because it all starts there. Harnessing hope matters.

TAKE ACTION

HIGH: Inspire hope. Get a group and have each person write five to ten notes of hope. Then post your notes in random places in your community. Maybe the freezer case at your local grocery store, on the windshield of a parked car, or on your seat while exiting a plane.

MEDIUM: Create a "Wall of Hope." Write what you hope for on Post-its or paper bricks. Post the messages of hope on a wall that people pass by often to help inspire hope in others. Offer supplies near your wall, so anyone who visits can add their hopes as well.

LOW: Create a hopeful affirmation to say to yourself every day. It can be specific to something you are currently focused on tackling, or it can be something more general and universal, like "I am hopeful." Just make sure to say it often.

> **WHEN THE WORLD SAYS, "GIVE UP," HOPE WHISPERS, "TRY IT ONE MORE TIME."**
>
> — Anonymous

97

TAKE ACTION

HIGH: Offer to be a mentor to someone who needs a person in their corner. Set up a regular time to meet. Help them focus, hear them out, and provide your support and wisdom in small and meaningful doses. Then get out of the way and watch them soar.

MEDIUM: Reach out to someone who believed in you and made a real difference in your life. Call, write a note, or email them. If possible, spend one-on-one time with them to share the significance of the belief in yourself they gave you and how it shaped you.

LOW: Are you holding yourself back by not believing in yourself? Reflect on your self-doubts. Think of the actions you can take or words you can use to build yourself up rather than tear yourself down. If it helps, post a few affirmation notes where you'll see them every day.

> ## CELEBRATE THE SUCCESS OF OTHERS. HIGH TIDE FLOATS ALL SHIPS.
>
> —Susan Elizabeth Phillips

We are powerful beings in many ways. With just a single word or endearing gesture, we can change someone's day in an instant. This simple phenomenon is so profound, it even works with total strangers. When we dig in even further, we can begin to embrace how important it is to **BELIEVE IN OTHERS**. Most likely, at some point in your life, you had someone who always believed in you. Maybe it was a family member, coach, teacher, or friend. Because of that person, you were able to soar to new heights, conquer a fear, or become a better version of yourself. They listened without being distracted. They loved you at your best and your worst. They inspired you, even when you didn't believe in yourself. They held on tighter, even when you tried your best to push them away. Well, what if all of us embraced this role? What if we all had someone who said we were the one who believed in him or her, and it made all the difference in their world? Well, we can and we should. And I believe we can do it. How's that for belief? Believing in others matters.

MONDAY GETS EXPRESSIVE

Everyone has a story, and everyone's story is unique. It's our stories that make us who we are today, because it is our life experiences—the good, the bad, and the ugly ones—that shape our beliefs and feelings about ourselves, others, and humanity at large. But the question we need to answer is whether we have allowed people to really know our stories. Do we let people in far enough, or do we dodge and weave our way through life with only the masks we want others to see? Have we built a facade of who we are and how we feel on social media in order to share a story that looks perfect? Only you know the answer to these questions, but my hope is that you are ready to openly offer your truest self to the world. Why? Because you matter and you are perfect just the way you are. Get vulnerable, be honest and authentic, and trust that you will be embraced for everything that makes you...you. We all get one life to live, so let's live it as our true selves and not someone else. Being expressive matters.

MEAN YOUR MESSAGE

We are now living in what is termed the post-truth era. People say what they want, whenever they want, wherever they want, even if it is untrue—or, dare I say, a flat-out provable lie. No, not just little white lies with minimal impact, rather major lies that are literally destroying the moral fabric of society and breaking down trust in our relationships and institutions. We throw around words with no moral compass, accountability, or regard for the damage they may cause. No longer are the days of Honest Abe, when you and I were only as good as our word. It's time to stop the madness and raise the bar back up. This week, truly **MEAN YOUR MESSAGE**. Your words and actions are powerful. They can tear someone down or lift someone up. They can encourage goodness and positivity in the world, or they can fan the flames of hate and negativity. Knowing we have the ability to use our words for good, why would we ever choose the opposite? Let's think before we speak and act. And if we can't do this, then just know that some messages are better left unsaid. Meaning your message matters.

TAKE ACTION

HIGH: Conduct a personal-message audit. Go back over your last few days' social media posts, emails, and/or replay some conversations you've had. Did you mean every word? Did they spread positivity or negativity? Be honest with yourself in your personal audit, then pledge to make any necessary adjustments.

MEDIUM: Try the old "dollar every time you _____" system for yourself or a team. Every time someone gossips, lies, speaks thoughtlessly, or is negative, they add a dollar into the jar. Donate the money to a good cause, and see what you can learn from this experience.

LOW: Be mindful of your messages and words this week. Choose them carefully and only share messages that you know are true. Carefully choose positive and constructive words that help convey your messages successfully.

> **PEOPLE MAY HEAR YOUR WORDS, BUT THEY FEEL YOUR ATTITUDE.**
>
> —John C. Maxwell

SHARE A SECRET

TAKE ACTION

HIGH: Reflect on your deepest and most difficult secrets today. Explore where and when those secrets started, why you are still holding on to them, and which ones might be better finally shared with those you trust most.

MEDIUM: Swap some secrets with your inner circle. Have everyone write down one secret they're ready to share on a slip of paper. Once a secret has been read aloud, either have fun with guessing whose secret it is or just let it stay anonymous—at least it was shared.

LOW: Share a secret from your childhood with someone special in your life. It may have hurt back then, but hopefully you can now have a good laugh and feel even better about how far you've come.

> THE MAN WHO CAN KEEP A SECRET MAY BE WISE, BUT HE IS NOT HALF AS WISE AS THE MAN WITH NO SECRETS TO KEEP.
>
> —E. W. Howe

Our secrets are our sickness. Sure, we have all been asked to keep a secret, but those are not the secrets I am talking about here. I mean the ones that only we know about, because they are our own little private secrets. The ones that we hide, because we know they would be uncomfortable and unpleasant for someone to hear and for us to share. They haunt us and make us insecure, untrusting…sick. So in the spirit of being expressive and healthy, it's time to **SHARE A SECRET**. Now, before you go spilling the beans everywhere, we need to be smart about this. While some of our secrets may be silly, like an embarrassing story or a fear of clowns, others need to be handled with care. We need to have a trusted tribe around us, or even a professional, in order to share them safely. These secrets are the most challenging yet most important ones to let out, so be bold and go for it. The more we share, the more we connect with one another, the more we live authentically, and the more we can help each other heal. Sharing your secrets matters.

THIS WEEK...
CHERISH LOVE

Abraham Maslow's theory of human motivation tells us that, before anything else, we need air, food, shelter, water, law, safety, and security. But isn't it interesting that as soon as we have those needs met, our next most significant need is love? Love lets us know we matter and that someone cares about us. It also allows us to make sure that people we care about feel the exact same way. So this week, let's **CHERISH LOVE**. We all experienced love before we were even born, when our mothers carried us in their wombs. With our first breath, we received our first loving touch—an immediate sense of acceptance, trust, intimacy, and safety. And as we grew older, we dated, and we knew every word to every number one love song on the radio. We were taught to be kind and to embrace our family, friends, and neighbors. We were all probably also hurt by love, because nothing hurts us more than love. But that's only because we loved in the first place. So let's love deeper, with greater sincerity, and more often. Let's make sure everyone in our lives knows how much we love them. Cherishing love matters.

TAKE ACTION

HIGH: There are many people in our communities that might not feel truly loved. They might be homeless, incarcerated, living in an elderly community, or farming our fruits and vegetables. Work with those you love to find ways to express love to these people who just might need it most.

MEDIUM: Make every day Valentine's Day! Who needs some love? Is it your partner, a best friend, a parent, a teacher, a coach, an aunt or uncle, your son or daughter, or even a sibling? All of the above? Share your love in your own creative and meaningful way.

LOW: Give yourself a loving hug. Take a deep breath and exhale, and while you do, say "I love you" to you. You can't love another until you learn to love yourself first. A little self-love goes a long way toward feeling good and being ready to spread the love.

> **THE MOST IMPORTANT THING IN THE WORLD IS FAMILY AND LOVE.**
>
> — John Wooden

BE A FLATTERER

TAKE ACTION

HIGH: Compliments, Post-it Notes, and a Sharpie make for a perfect compliment trifecta. You are now armed and dangerous, in a great way. You know what you need to do next.

MEDIUM: Write down five compliments that, if someone said them to you, would mean the world to you. Then share them more often. Not just with yourself but with other people in your life, knowing your words will most likely mean just as much to them as they do to you.

LOW: Spend a few moments thinking about how you receive or react to people's compliments of you. If it is something you struggle with, ask yourself why and come up with some strategies to retrain yourself to welcome those compliments. Trust me, you are worthy of them.

> IT WOULD BE FLATTERING TO BE THOUGHT OF AS SOMEONE WHO CELEBRATED LIFE.
>
> —Björk

How do you feel when someone gives you a compliment? Does it make you feel uncomfortable, or do you openly receive their kind words and feel good in the moment? If you're not sure how to answer that, then think about this: When someone gives you a compliment, how do you respond? Do you warmly say "Thank you," or do you immediately reply with a compliment for them or try to downplay or deflect their compliment? I have a hunch as to what answers are coming up for you, so this week, it's time for all of us to **BE A FLATTERER**. Before we can change the world, we all need to get super comfortable giving and receiving compliments. If we can't happily exchange niceties, the rest of the work simply can't happen. So imagine over seven billion people waking up every day with the sole purpose of lifting one another up. Talk about a game changer. So let me get this started: Thank you for buying this book and putting it to work in your life. Hopefully that didn't make you feel too uncomfortable, because I really meant it. Just say "Thank you" and pay it forward. Being a flatterer matters.

MONDAY GETS RESILIENT

"It's not how many times you get knocked down. It's how many times you get back up." "It's not the cards you are dealt, rather how you play them." Sayings, mantras, quotes...all spouting advice on standing tall, being strong, and brushing it off. It's as if we are all supposed to be superheroes, equipped with superpowers that allow us to deflect any challenge or evil that comes our way. Kind of a cool idea, but we have to remember that behind every superhero is a normal, everyday person—someone more like us. We live, love, laugh, cry, hurt, and struggle. Life can be very real and a bit messy, and, unfortunately, we can't just turn green or jump into a phone booth to make it all go away. Nor should we want that to be the case. But we can honor our feelings, express ourselves, be mindful, and trust that tomorrow will be a new day. We all have the power to rise to the occasion and pave a new path. It just takes some courage and belief that anything is possible. Being resilient matters.

INVITE FEEDBACK

Feedback is a tricky thing. We need feedback to learn, to be dialed in. It is honest feedback from trusted people that allows us to grow. But even though we know feedback is a good thing, it doesn't mean it's always easy to ask for or receive it. In fact, sometimes it can be quite difficult to hear, which is why it makes sense that we don't ask for it very often. It's that whole touching-the-hot-stove thing again. But shouldn't it be everyone's responsibility—and hopefully desire—to constantly improve and to become the best versions of ourselves? I think and hope so. So let's make this week all about **INVITING FEEDBACK**. Maybe it is feedback from a colleague or a classmate. Maybe it is from a friend or family member. We all have different roles we fulfill throughout our day, and most of them depend on interacting with other people. In other words, there is plenty of access for feedback; we just need to invite it. Just make sure to only ask people who will deliver it honestly and from a place of love and growth, not judgment or hurt. Inviting honest feedback matters.

TAKE ACTION

HIGH: Make feedback a "we thing" by conducting a few rounds of "fishbowl feedback." Take turns sharing one positive piece of feedback about one person in the group. Then conduct a second round with each person sharing a piece of constructive feedback along with the benefits of trying that suggestion.

MEDIUM: Write down the different roles you play throughout your day—spouse, classmate, friend, etc. Then find at least one person for each of those roles that you can go to for feedback. Make sure to give them permission to say no or ask for more time first.

LOW: Create three columns to explore your goals/roles. At the top of the first column, write "Keep Doing." Then write "Stop Doing" at the top of the second column, and "Start Doing" at the top of the third column. Now, review your roles and goals, sorting between the columns.

> # WE ALL NEED PEOPLE WHO WILL GIVE US FEEDBACK. THAT'S HOW WE IMPROVE.
>
> — Bill Gates

BE A BOUNCER

TAKE ACTION

HIGH: Has something happened to you that was hard to bounce back from? Make a choice today to really examine it and to notice how it impacts who you are. Then make a plan to work through it and to start feeling better.

MEDIUM: Do you know someone who needs a little help bouncing back from a setback? See what you can do to offer some support in the form of what's-important-is-what-you-do-about-it-and-learn-from-it advice. Lead with love and kindness and commit to being there to help them get to the other side.

LOW: Look at some of the simple negative things that happen to you and take notice of how you respond to them. This is that parking ticket you just got, the long line at the grocery store, or those cold french fries you were just served. Do you wallow or bounce?

> I AM NOT WHAT HAPPENED TO ME. I AM WHAT I CHOOSE TO BECOME.
>
> —Anonymous

Are you a bouncer? No, not someone who works as a security guard. I mean someone who bounces back easily. Or are you a wallower—someone who likes to hang out in the muddiness of things and embrace your inner victim? Of course, there is nothing wrong with feeling your real emotions, but part of being resilient also means moving forward. In other words, it means bouncing back. So this week, I want to empower you to **BE A BOUNCER**. Even with all of our dreams and desires to live a fulfilling, happy, and pain-free life, it doesn't always go that way. There is the simple stuff, like parking tickets, rude customers, or a leaky faucet. Then there are the more challenging ones, like being let go by your employer, losing a friend or family member, or unintentionally letting someone down. Whether we want to accept it or not, all of these things will happen during our lifetimes. No one is 100 percent immune. So we are all left with a choice. Will we be bouncers or wallowers? We can't control everything that happens to us, but we can control how we respond to it. Bouncing back matters.

CHOOSE WISELY

The average adult makes over 35,000 choices per day. That's over 245,000 choices per week, 1 million per month, and 12 million per year. No wonder our heads hurt every now and then. But just because we make 12 million choices per year, we can't take for granted the significance of any of them. Yes, just like voting, every choice matters. Our choices reflect who we are, and they shape how our lives and the lives of others will unfold. So this week, let's make sure to **CHOOSE WISELY**. How do you make decisions? Do you have certain criteria or a clear understanding of how you process your choices? Do you really own how your choices affect your life? We can choose to call for a ride, or we can drink and drive. We can surround ourselves with healthy relationships, or we can operate with blinders on. We can eat healthily, get plenty of exercise, and rest, or we can live an unhealthy life. Making sense? When we make the right choices, the situations that require resiliency naturally decrease. When we don't, being resilient becomes a skill we need even more. Choosing wisely matters.

YOU ARE FREE TO CHOOSE, BUT YOU ARE NOT FREE FROM THE CONSEQUENCE OF YOUR CHOICE.

—Anonymous

TAKE ACTION

HIGH: Think of the impact of your choices. For example, maybe you don't exercise, and doing it for your own health isn't motivating. Well, think about how your health impacts those around you. You have people in your life who love and need you, so choose to be healthy for them.

MEDIUM: Create a criterion for how you make choices. Consider the morals and values that drive your choices so you have something concrete to help you make consistent and constructive choices.

LOW: Who can you help make better choices without being a know-it-all? Be there for a friend or family member, and supportively present their choices in simple terms. They'll grow stronger with every choice they make for the better, and you'll be glad you made the choice to help.

117

PLAY THE HERO

TAKE ACTION

HIGH: Organize a band of heroes for guerrilla-style volunteering. Be open to something simple and organic, like cleaning up a park or bus stop on a random day. Put it out there to your posse o' heroes and achieve greatness. Start today.

MEDIUM: Find a picture of a hero you admire. It makes no difference if it's a fictional hero or a real star. Just be sure your chosen person embodies strong qualities. Post their picture somewhere you will see it on a regular basis for a daily dose of inspiration.

LOW: Who needs you to be their hero right now? Answer the call.

> **EVERYONE IS NECESSARILY THE HERO OF HIS OWN LIFE STORY.**
>
> —John Barth

Every classic story has a few main characters—the villain, the victim, and the hero. Really good stories have a way of connecting us to each of the characters. But now, consider your life and imagine it as its own classic story. After all, you do have a story. What character are you playing? I hope it's not the villain. We certainly know that the victim thing doesn't really work. So what's left? Yes, you guessed it. It's time to **PLAY THE HERO**. Unfortunately, our world has plenty of villains and victims already but seemingly never enough heroes. One might argue that our world is in need of heroes now more than ever. But being a hero shouldn't be something that's larger than life. All we need to do is become hyper-aware of opportunities where we can serve one another. Give someone a call, volunteer, smile, or go the extra mile by surprising your neighbors by washing their car or offering to babysit. The deed may be small but the impact mighty. A world filled with ordinary heroes serving one another and the greater good can overcome any challenges that come its way. Playing the hero matters.

MONDAY GETS KIND

Kindness is magic. You know it when you see it. You know it when you receive it. You know it when you extend it. Kindness alone can change the world. It is one of the few things in life that literally changes everything, which is pretty remarkable when you consider that it can be something so simple and small, yet so powerful and profound. The only question this month asks us to answer is whether we are ready for it, because kindness is a choice. I think it should be the only choice. Anything we experience in our relationships, see during the day, read online, or watch on TV that has any negativity associated with it is because someone didn't choose kindness. Instead, they chose hate, power, money, apathy, disregard, or selfishness. But who wants a world that results from those choices? Not me. So let's be bold and brave enough to create a kinder world. How? By being more kind. Imagine a multiple-choice question with only one answer, *kindness*. Yes, this means that it is more powerful to be *kind* than *right*. Think you can handle it? Your call. Kindness matters.

After every holiday, birthday, wedding, or just-because event, we are all faced with an important decision. We didn't necessarily ask for it, but we secretly kind of like it, because it means we were the recipients of someone's kindness. It might have been in the form of flowers, a wrapped gift, a delicious dinner, a gift card, or simply a special sharing of someone's heart. In such moments, we can either reciprocate the kindness or just keep it all for ourselves. I like the former, so welcome to **GIVE THANKS** week. Whether you say, text, or write it, giving thanks is one of the most powerful ways to show kindness. It just takes those two magic words: Thank you. Yet as simple as it is, it is also pretty easy to let slip by day after day. Once it gets to week after week or month after month, we avoid saying it simply to avoid feeling embarrassed. Well, it doesn't matter if it's been a week, a month, or even longer. It's never too late to say thank you, because showing genuine kindness and appreciation always matters. So thank you for reading this, and thank you for saying thank you.

WHEN YOU LEARN TO SAY THANK YOU, YOU SEE THE WORLD ANEW.

—Oprah Winfrey

TAKE ACTION

HIGH: Coordinate a "thank-you-card-a-thon." Get together with a group of coworkers, friends, or family to create thank-you cards for service members, veterans, first responders, and even your friendly, local garbage collectors or mail delivery people. Let's show appreciation to those who make our lives so much safer and better.

MEDIUM: Get back into the habit of saying thank you as often as possible. Thank the person who drops off your mail, makes your coffee, holds the door for you, and most of all, the person you can count on to be there for you each and every day.

LOW: Find someone special you really want to show your appreciation for and share your thanks with them with a little added flair. Get creative and go the extra mile. They will love it, and you know they deserve it.

LISTEN FIRST

TAKE ACTION

HIGH: Organize a workshop or attend a local seminar on effective listening. Invite colleagues, friends, or family members to attend as well so you can all benefit. Afterward, spend time practicing your listening skills with one another to help build stronger relationships.

MEDIUM: Track down a few TED Talks or other inspirational videos on the importance and power of listening. Put into practice any cool tips you learn from those who have dedicated their lives to helping others get better at the art of listening.

LOW: Take a friend or family member out to lunch with the sole purpose of being there to listen. Ask a few questions to get them started and then listen to their story. The power of listening is truly empowering to both the one who is listened to and the listener.

> WE HAVE TWO EARS AND ONE MOUTH SO THAT WE CAN LISTEN TWICE AS MUCH AS WE SPEAK.
>
> —Epictetus

"So, I was thinki…"

"You know, wha…"

"I would lov…"

Ever been in a situation when you were trying to say something and someone wouldn't let you finish your sentence? How about when you were saying something and, at the same time, someone else started saying something to you, and it became a game of who can say it the loudest? Both cases are great examples of a communication breakdown, a.k.a. interrupting. Interrupting sucks. It says that your feelings, thoughts, and words don't matter. There is nothing kind about that. So this week, let's choose to **LISTEN FIRST**. Easy, right? Well, maybe not. Please hear me out for a second. Nowadays, listening does not come naturally to us. We get distracted by our phones, our thoughts, and formulating our replies. If that is not bad enough, we also still expect people to listen to what we have to say. Oh, the irony of it all. Let's get back to being kind and honoring one another through active listening. Be present, engage, look them in the eye, and acknowledge their words and sentiments. It's the only way we can all be heard. Listening first matters.

THIS WEEK...
RIPPLE KINDNESS

Whether you truly embrace this or not, you are constantly impacting those around you. They watch how you treat other people, how you drive, your facial expressions, and they listen to your words...even when you are not talking to them. See, being known is not just for celebrities; you are famous in your own right. You're a role model. So this week, make sure to **RIPPLE KINDNESS**. Somehow, kindness has become most associated with being a random act. Something that is both rare and unexpected, so it gets celebrated on social media. #RAK gets a lot of love these days. But what does this say about kindness and our culture? Shouldn't kindness be the norm? And is a kind act really random, anyway? I don't think so. I believe that kind acts are intentional. They start as an idea in someone's mind, and then they act on it. I also believe that we should always expect kindness from ourselves and from other people. In other words, it shouldn't surprise us because of its rarity. So let's start a new hashtag, #AK, meaning "Always Kind," and let that ripple out into the world. Rippling kindness matters.

WHEREVER THERE IS A HUMAN BEING, THERE IS AN OPPORTUNITY FOR A KINDNESS.

—Lucius Annaeus Seneca

TAKE ACTION

HIGH: Think about someone in your life who you know could use a big dose of love and kindness. Make it your mission this week to shower them with it. Remember, you have the ability to change a life. That's powerful stuff.

MEDIUM: Start a kindness campaign at home or work. Ask everyone to join the campaign by writing down every kind thing they do this week and adding them to a community jar. At the end of the week, celebrate all the kindness you were able to ripple into the world.

LOW: Every morning this week, say to yourself that you are going to be on constant lookout for moments where you can ripple kindness. Get ready for a super kind week.

THIS WEEK...
HUG OUR MOTHERS

TAKE ACTION

HIGH: Participate in or organize a community cleanup day. Find ways to get local companies, schools, churches, friends, and family members to join in. Make it fun and a day for everyone to show kindness to our mothers. Picking up litter is good; having no litter to pick up is better.

MEDIUM: Reduce. Of all the *R*'s—Reduce, Reuse, Recycle—reduce is the best option. Take shorter showers, print on both sides, carpool, change your sprinkler timers, etc. You know these ideas already. Now you just have to do them. The planet and your pocketbook will love you.

LOW: Be kind to animals. Take time to research how humans are impacting the different species from around the world—from dolphins to elephants to orang-utans to factory-farm animals. Brace yourself. You won't see a ton of kindness in your searches, but this is the very reason to get involved.

THE FUTURE WILL EITHER BE GREEN OR NOT AT ALL.

—Bob Brown

There are endless facts to prove that we humans negatively impact our planet. I agree that knowing the statistics and the science is important. However, I also believe that this can easily distract us from the real root of the problem. Our environment is not a scientific issue; it's a human one. All those stats are just the symptoms resulting from the lack of respect and kindness we have for one another and our planet. So this week, let's get honest with ourselves. It's time to **HUG OUR MOTHERS**—Earth and Nature, that is. We know enough and we know better, so the fact that we are still not doing enough is no longer a problem of pollution but a more personal problem. We can argue whether there's really nine or eight or seven billion tons of litter in our oceans, but we run out of arguments when we all know that littering just one single piece of paper is where it all starts. So let's focus on the real issue. Our planet doesn't pollute itself. That's on us. And it's time for us to choose kindness. Hugging Mother Earth and Mother Nature matters.

MONDAY GETS INTROSPECTIVE

SEARCH YOUR SOUL   2

JOURNAL ENTRY
What is one thing that you feel your soul yearns for the most, and how can you bring this into your life? You might need to write out a "soul plan" and break down the steps you will need to take.

CONVERSATION STARTER
If you were to interview your soul, how would it answer the following questions: What is your guiding light? What do you need more or less of? What other questions would you like to ask your soul?

HAVE A DREAM   4

JOURNAL ENTRY
When you close your eyes, what dreams feel most important and are most vivid in your mind? What do they include? Fill in as many details as you can. How does that feel? How can you help yourself or someone else realize this bright vision?

CONVERSATION STARTER
What is a dream of yours that you hope people will still believe in over fifty years from now? On the flipside, what is another dream that you hope will become a reality before fifty years from now?

BE IN AWE 6

JOURNAL ENTRY
In what ways can you be more tuned in to the many awe-inspiring moments in your daily life? What's one awesome thing you would like to experience tomorrow? How can you make that happen?

CONVERSATION STARTER
What is something awesome you experienced today? How did that thing make you feel when you experienced it? How does it make you feel now?

LIVE AUTHENTICALLY 8

JOURNAL ENTRY
In what areas of your life do you find yourself compromising due to your lack of courage to be yourself or your willingness to speak your truth? Why do you continue to make those choices, and how can you be more honest with yourself and others?

CONVERSATION STARTER
What is a truth you've been holding back? How can you share this truth with yourself and others?

MONDAY GETS AMBITIOUS

PLAN YOUR PLAN 12

JOURNAL ENTRY

Think of a realistic goal you can achieve in one month, then create a quick plan for it. Then do it eleven more times. You just created a plan to accomplish twelve mini, month-long goals this year. Doesn't that sound amazing? Enjoy your uber productive year.

CONVERSATION STARTER

What is one goal that you have always wanted to achieve but never made a proper plan to make it a reality? Are you ready to go for it? How can you create a plan that you can follow through on?

FAIL AT SOMETHING 14

JOURNAL ENTRY

Ask yourself this simple question: Are you living a life designed around not failing? If yes, how is this holding you back in your life? Think about how you can shift your attitude and beliefs around failing, even if it's only in one area of your life. Then write yourself a pep talk that helps you psych up to face this fear of failure. Next step: face it.

CONVERSATION STARTER

What is something you tried to achieve but failed at? How did you handle that failure at first? How did that failure help you grow and have a positive impact on you in the end? Did you go back and try again? What happened?

GET ENERGIZED 16

JOURNAL ENTRY

Each day, for the next five days, draw a graph that plots your energy levels throughout the day. Think lows and highs and how your energy varied throughout each day. After five days, see if you discover any trends. Do you see drops throughout the day? Recognize what triggered them and how you can avoid them moving forward.

CONVERSATION STARTER

If you were a boxer or mixed martial artist, what song would you play as you enter the arena?

BE YOUR OWN BIGGEST FAN 18

JOURNAL ENTRY

Make two lists: "Things I love about myself" and "Things I don't love about myself." For every "don't love" item, move it to the "love" list by reframing it. For example: "Gray hair"—"I have experience and wisdom on my side." You get the drill.

CONVERSATION STARTER

If you were to give yourself an award for something you did today, this week, or this year, what would it be for and why? What would you want your Lifetime Achievement Award to be for?

MONDAY GETS JOYFUL

PLAY MORE   22

JOURNAL ENTRY
How does the idea of having more play time and playfulness in your life feel? What's getting in the way of your having that time now? How are you going to overcome those challenges and experience more joy through play?

CONVERSATION STARTER
What were some of your favorite games to play when you were a child? Why were those your favorites? Are you ready to play them again? Then make a date to recapture that childhood fun.

LAUGH TILL IT HURTS   24

JOURNAL ENTRY
Write down five things that you know make you laugh and bring you joy. Now go down your list and laugh till it hurts.

CONVERSATION STARTER
Who is the funniest comedian of all time? What is the funniest movie of all? Get ready to make your case.

ADD COLOR 26

JOURNAL ENTRY
How can you add more color to your own life and the lives of others? Get specific.

CONVERSATION STARTER
If you had to pick one color to describe yourself, what color would it be and why?

LOVE THE LITTLE THINGS 28

JOURNAL ENTRY
How many little things that bring you joy can you list? Go for it. Don't be afraid to keep adding to your list in the days, weeks, and years ahead. Here's to a lifetime of little joyful moments.

CONVERSATION STARTER
What is something little that happened to you this week that brought you joy? Did you notice it at the time? What can you do to love the little things more often?

MONDAY GETS SELFLESS

GO SECOND 32

JOURNAL ENTRY
Do you think that the result is more important than the journey? Write about how you've taken this approach in your own life for better or worse. How can you learn to value the journey, even if it means taking a back seat to others' needs at points along the way?

CONVERSATION STARTER
Why are we so competitive these days? How do you see this playing out in your world? How can we reverse those trends by putting others first more often?

DO WITHOUT 34

JOURNAL ENTRY
What and where can you cut back on your spending so you can give more to others? Less on junk food? Less on clothes? Less on eating out? Create a cut-back and give-back budget, and see how much your "doing without" provides you and others in return.

CONVERSATION STARTER
Do you have a certain thing that you have way too many of? How would it feel to donate half or more of them to someone who could use them? Think you can do it? Will you?

CONSPIRE FOR GOOD   36

JOURNAL ENTRY

Create a "conspiring for good" personal plan. Each of us has
1,440 minutes per day, 10,080 minutes per week, and 525,600
minutes per year. How many of these minutes are you willing
to use for doing good? Is it 1 percent, 5 percent, 10 percent?
Once you know your number, create your action plan and start
conspiring for good.

CONVERSATION STARTER

Do you think that giving or doing acts of good is selfish or
selfless? Why do you think that?

SMILE AT A STRANGER   38

JOURNAL ENTRY

Take a minute to smile at yourself in the mirror, then sketch a
picture of your smile and write a description of it. What is unique
about it? What does it communicate? If you had to give it a
name, what would it be? Then list a few of the special ways you
love to share your smile with others.

CONVERSATION STARTER

Share a story when a smile from someone, even a stranger,
brightened up the day for you. Why did it have such an impact
on you?

MONDAY GETS QUIET

UNPLUG 42

JOURNAL ENTRY

Map out your personal electronic grid and how much time you spend on each device in your map. Make sure to include all electronics you use. Now create a plan to unplug and list at three new healthy habits you will form with your newfound time.

CONVERSATION STARTER

How much would someone have to pay you to take your phone away for one hour, five hours, one day, or one week? What would you do with all that free time?

KNOW YOUR EMOTIONS 44

JOURNAL ENTRY

Draw a chart with two columns. On the left side, write down five words that you would like people to use to describe you. Then, on the right side, write down five words that describe how you feel inside. If the words on the right side don't align with those on the left, know that it's OK to not always feel OK. What matters is how we respond to those feelings.

CONVERSATION STARTER

What was one of the most challenging emotional experiences in your life so far? Is it still hard to think about it? How have your grown from it? How has it shaped you into the person you are today? How does this affect how you support others during their rough patches?

GET OUTDOORS 46

JOURNAL ENTRY

Where do you love to experience nature? How can you get out there to breathe it all in more often? Draw a few pictures, print a few off the internet, and add them to these pages. Let them inspire you to make a get-outdoors commitment to yourself. Even once a month is better than nothing, but hopefully you can make it happen more often than that.

CONVERSATION STARTER

If you could choose to be outdoors right this very second, where would it be and what would you be doing? How would you feel?

SAY NO TO SAY YES 48

JOURNAL ENTRY

On a scale of 1 to 10, with 10 being high, how much of a people pleaser are you? In what ways does this work and not work in your life? What could be some pros and cons to making adjustments that help put yourself first a bit more often? While you are at it, write down some things you would like to do with your newly created me time as you become a little more of a me pleaser too.

CONVERSATION STARTER

Are you good at saying yes to yourself and no to others, or is it the other way around for you? If it's the latter, what's so hard about saying no, and how can you change that? If you're good at the yes-to-you thing, what advice can you offer others who want to improve?

MONDAY GETS HUMAN

TAKE THE HIGH ROAD

JOURNAL ENTRY

How can you live and act in the spirit of taking the high road? How can you inspire others to do the same?

CONVERSATION STARTER

Share stories about when you took the high road, but be 100 percent honest on how the decision process went for you. Was it easy? What were your honest thoughts? Don't worry. You took the high road in the end, so share your truth.

PRIORITIZE PEOPLE

JOURNAL ENTRY

Who are the people in your life you want to prioritize more than you're doing right now? How can you make it happen for them and you?

CONVERSATION STARTER

What gets in the way of prioritizing people? What little or big actions can we take to reprioritize the people in our lives and community?

FORGIVE FREELY 56

JOURNAL ENTRY

Do you forgive easily? Why or why not? How can you help yourself forgive more freely? Who and for what can you start with? Then keep going.

CONVERSATION STARTER

Can you recall a time when you forgave someone, even though it was hard to do so, or when someone forgave you for something you did? How did that act of forgiveness make a difference in your lives?

PRACTICE PATIENCE 58

JOURNAL ENTRY

List any pet peeves you have that test your patience. Then write down ideas about how you can better handle those encounters. After all, we know they will happen again.

CONVERSATION STARTER

Share a story where you totally lost your patience. What did you learn from it? How would you handle it differently if it happened again?

MONDAY GETS CREATIVE

BE IN ART AWE   62

JOURNAL ENTRY
Think of a work of art that you love or find a picture of it to put in
your journal. Then write down what it means to you and why you
find it so special. If you are really feeling it, draw a sketch of the
work to go along with your narrative.

CONVERSATION STARTER
If you could make a living as an artist, what type of art would you
create? Why?

BUILD SOMETHING   64

JOURNAL ENTRY
Trace both of your hands and fill them in with all the things you
do with them. Then leave an empty space somewhere to write
one thing you are committing to build with your hands this week
or month. Your hands just got even more talented right before
your eyes.

CONVERSATION STARTER
Of every structure, piece of art, or invention ever built or created
by hand, which marvels you the most and why?

SURPRISE THE WORLD   66

JOURNAL ENTRY

Write out a list of people in your life who you want to surprise this year. Then start coming up with and writing down your creative surprise ideas. Just make sure they don't have access to your journal.

CONVERSATION STARTER

What is the best surprise someone has ever done for you or you did for someone else? How did that surprise make the surprisee and surpriser feel in the end?

ENJOY VARIETY   68

JOURNAL ENTRY

We have all heard of bucket lists; well, how about a variety list? Now you have. Write a list of ten new things or experiences you want to try, then get to checking them off.

CONVERSATION STARTER

What is something you tried for the very first time and absolutely loved? Was it a food? A new hobby? An exercise class? How did the whole experience unfold?

MONDAY GETS CONNECTED

CONNECT TO COMMUNITY 72

JOURNAL ENTRY

Write a travel bureau sales piece about your community. Think of it as something that a potential tourist would read to see if they were interested in visiting. The fate of your community's tourism industry is in your hands. No pressure.

CONVERSATION STARTER

What is a hidden gem that you absolutely love doing or visiting in your community? What makes it so special?

GET A GROUP 74

JOURNAL ENTRY

Write "My People" at the top of your page. Then write down and fill in these ten phrases: *I can try new things with _____. _____ listens to me. I can cry with _____. I can laugh with _____. _____ is always honest with me. _____ helps me grow. I can trust _____ with anything. I can travel with _____. I have similar hobbies to _____ . _____ shares similar beliefs about life.* If no one comes to mind, then you just set a new goal for yourself to meet someone who does. Or if many of your statements only get one name, or it is the same person over and over again, you just set another goal for yourself: to broaden your circle.

CONVERSATION STARTER

What does the saying "You have to be a friend to have a friend" mean to you?

FIND COMMON GROUND 76

JOURNAL ENTRY
Write down any labels you use or have used in the past that don't serve you or someone else well. It's OK to be super honest with yourself here. Now imagine those labels disappearing from the page. If you wrote them in pencil, erase them. If you used a pen, then scribble them out. Trust you'll be better off without them.

CONVERSATION STARTER
How can we as a society do a better job of celebrating what makes us different and unique in a way that further connects us?

MAKE THE FIRST MOVE 78

JOURNAL ENTRY
How has having a cell phone with you at all times hindered your ability to connect with people in your immediate surroundings? How could you wean yourself off that phone and look up and engage more often?

CONVERSATION STARTER
Do you talk to people in elevators or in line at the grocery store? Why or why not? What's the funniest make-the-first-move experience you've ever had, whether you were the first mover or someone else was?

MONDAY GETS AWARE

SEEK EQUALITY 82

JOURNAL ENTRY

Research some of the inequalities that exist in the world today, and pick one to champion. For example, maybe you are a vegan and don't believe there is such a thing as cruelty-free meat. Do your research, take notes, then create a plan for how you and others can help.

CONVERSATION STARTER

Of all the injustices and inequalities in the world, what is the one you are most passionate about, and what are you doing to make a positive impact? What more do you think you can do to "be the change"?

OWN IT 84

JOURNAL ENTRY

Ask and answer this question in your journal more often: What am I not owning? What can I do to make things better now that I've acknowledged this, and how can I start taking more ownership?

CONVERSATION STARTER

What do you think Michael Jackson meant when he wrote and sang, "I'm starting with the man in the mirror"? What do you see when you look in the mirror, when it comes to you owning it?

KNOW YOUR ROOTS 86

JOURNAL ENTRY
You have been assigned to write a blog on your family's history. Think about everyone you will need to interview and what questions you want to ask them. Of course, once your interviews are finished, write the piece, and share it with your family.

CONVERSATION STARTER
What is one of your favorite stories that a family member from an older generation shared with you?

TRACK YOUR TIME 88

JOURNAL ENTRY
Keep a log of how you spend your time every day for a week. Write down all of the activities you do every day with how many minutes or hours you spend on each. Hint: the total number should be 168 hours. Once you have become way more aware, take a closer look at things you do that might be considered a waste of time, and replace them with what matters most to you.

CONVERSATION STARTER
If suddenly you were given a twenty-five-hour day, what would you do with that extra hour?

MONDAY GETS POSITIVE

FLIP THE SCRIPT

JOURNAL ENTRY

What negative scene do you see playing out over and over again in your own or someone else's life? Now write two TV scripts with these same characters and scenes in mind. The first is how you (and the people in your life) usually act out the negative plot. The second script is the positive one. Now reflect on the two stories, and see what you can do to make the positive script a true reality show.

CONVERSATION STARTER

What's an example of negative thinking you or those around you brought into this week? Now imagine you get a do-over on that thinking. How could you flip the script to something more positive for the upcoming week?

ASK "WHY NOT?"

JOURNAL ENTRY

Make a "Why not?" page in your journal for five things you want to accomplish in your lifetime. Add detail to your "Why not?" questions and start to imagine the steps you'll need to take on the way to checking them off your list. Remember, there's no deadline for making your big dreams come true.

CONVERSATION STARTER

Who comes to mind as someone who is not afraid to ask "Why not?" What has he or she accomplished or is accomplishing with this sort of mindset? How can you apply this same attitude and way of living for the betterment of your own life or the lives of others?

HARNESS HOPE   96

JOURNAL ENTRY

Are you a hopeful person? Why or why not? How can you harness hope to help yourself or others even more than you do today?

CONVERSATION STARTER

What do you hope for in the world? What are you doing to harness that hope and make it happen? Sorry, it can't be for three more wishes.

BELIEVE IN OTHERS   98

JOURNAL ENTRY

Who are the people in your life who have always believed in you? Who are the people you believe in? How can you thank the former and show more belief in the latter?

CONVERSATION STARTER

How do you show belief in others? What advice can you offer those who don't believe in themselves?

MONDAY GETS EXPRESSIVE

MEAN YOUR MESSAGE 102

JOURNAL ENTRY

What does truth mean to you? Where do you find yourself compromising the truth? What can you do to not compromise the truth while still being positive and constructive?

CONVERSATION STARTER

How does it feel knowing that we are now living in what is called the post-truth era? What role do we each have in taking back the truth and encouraging all of us to mean our messages?

SHARE A SECRET 104

JOURNAL ENTRY

Do you have a deep secret that you don't feel comfortable sharing yet? Then write about it instead. Include the what, why, when, and how this secret weighs on you personally and in your daily life. This might just be the first step to actually sharing it with someone you trust one day. If you don't feel comfortable having it in your journal, then rip it out after you are done and throw it away. Just make sure to shred it first.

CONVERSATION STARTER

What is the most embarrassing thing that has ever happened to you that you've never told anyone? How do you feel about that embarrassing moment now that you've shared it?

CHERISH LOVE

JOURNAL ENTRY

Think of a loved one with whom you would love to reconnect—literally or spiritually. Maybe it is a friend you miss terribly or even someone who passed away that you miss talking to. Then write this special person a love letter. Share what you have always wanted to say, or just express what you love or loved about them most. If the person you thought of is still alive, consider giving them the letter. If not, then create a special moment to read it aloud to them, believing they are listening to every single word.

CONVERSATION STARTER

What embodies true love on earth to you? Why and how does this represent love to you?

BE A FLATTERER

JOURNAL ENTRY

Make a list of people in your life who you know would love to receive a compliment from you. Then write out a compliment for each person on the list. The next time you connect with each of them, give them your compliment. It just might be that compliment they never forget.

CONVERSATION STARTER

What is a compliment that someone gave you that really made a big impact on you? Who would you like to share a compliment with as soon as possible and why?

MONDAY GETS RESILIENT

INVITE FEEDBACK 112

JOURNAL ENTRY
Spend some time thinking about the idea of feedback and answering a few of these questions: How does the thought of asking for feedback make you feel? Have you done it before? How did it go? If not, why not? How can you make asking for feedback a positive learning process for you?

CONVERSATION STARTER
Share a time when you received a piece of feedback that was tough to hear but that made a positive impact on your life. Who delivered it? Why did it sting? How did you show resiliency and learn from that feedback? How did it contribute to who you are today?

BE A BOUNCER 114

JOURNAL ENTRY
Do you have someone in your life who routinely puts or brings you down? Be specific with who they are and what they do to negatively impact you. Then create a plan to make it a healthier situation for yourself. Warning: this might mean bouncing them out. So many options, but wallowing is no longer one of them.

CONVERSATION STARTER
Are you a bouncer or a wallower? Why do you say that? How can you hone your bouncing skills even more?

CHOOSE WISELY   116

JOURNAL ENTRY
What is a choice that you seem to consistently make, knowing that it doesn't really serve your best interests? Now, what options are there for you to choose differently?

CONVERSATION STARTER
What are some choices you wish people would make more often than they do currently? Why do you think those choices are wiser? How can you encourage others to make these wiser choices?

PLAY THE HERO   118

JOURNAL ENTRY
Who is someone you know who you consider your hero or heroine? What makes them special? What qualities do they have that you aspire to develop over your lifetime? What can you do to become more like that special person you're thinking of?

CONVERSATION STARTER
When did you play the hero or heroine? What did you do? How did you help? How did that make you and others feel?

MONDAY GETS KIND

GIVE THANKS

122

JOURNAL ENTRY

Create a give-thanks system for yourself. Think about all the different ways someone has done something kind for you, both big and small. Then create five different go-to ways you can give thanks in response. Once you have your system in place, you will always be ready to give thanks immediately. Done.

CONVERSATION STARTER

When is the last time you received a thank-you note or card from someone? How did it make you feel? Who do you need to send a thank-you note to, and when will you make that happen?

LISTEN FIRST

124

JOURNAL ENTRY

On a scale of 1 to 10, with 10 being outstanding, how would you rate yourself when it comes to your listening skills? If improvement is needed, write down three things you will do to become a kinder and better listener. Now go listen away.

CONVERSATION STARTER

Share a story of when you were there to listen or when someone really listened to you and how it felt for everyone involved. How does that compare to the feeling of being interrupted or ignored?

RIPPLE KINDNESS   126

JOURNAL ENTRY

How would people in your life describe your special brand of kindness? What would they say you uniquely do to make the world a better place?

CONVERSATION STARTER

Who is someone you admire who started a ripple of kindness that had a profound impact on you and the world? What about them and what they did do you admire so much?

HUG OUR MOTHERS   128

JOURNAL ENTRY

What environmental causes are you passionate about? What will you commit to do in order to make a difference and improve the situation? "Nothing" doesn't work.

CONVERSATION STARTER

Why do you think people still debate whether we have environmental issues? How can we do a better job of connecting people to the importance of love and kindness when it comes to taking care of our planet?

ABOUT THE
AUTHOR

Matthew Emerzian is founder and chief inspiration officer of Every Monday Matters (EMM), a nonprofit organization committed to helping people and organizations understand how much and why they matter. Inspired by his book by the same name, EMM's programs have been utilized by some of America's largest corporations and over a million students in forty-nine states and seven countries. His work has been hailed by publications such as *Fast Company*, *Huffington Post*, and Oprah.com. Over the past ten years, Emerzian has traveled the country sharing his unique story and insight on finding purpose. His life-changing message focuses on sustained personal and social change that happens by stepping outside of ourselves by serving and connecting with one another. Prior to founding Every Monday Matters, Emerzian worked in the music industry as the senior vice president of Robert Kardashian's music company. He has managed and worked on projects with some of the largest acts in the world, including U2, Coldplay, Tim McGraw, Avril Lavigne, and Usher. Emerzian holds a master's degree from the Anderson School of Management at UCLA and resides with his wife, Patty Malcolm, and their rescue animals, Rooster, Rocky, and Rambo, in Hollywood, California.